SKI TOURING AND SNOWSHOEING IN THE DOLOMITES

50 WINTER ROUTES

About the Author

James Rushforth is an experienced and professional climber, mountaineer, skier and high-liner. His book *Rock Climbs and Via Ferrata – The Dolomites* was nominated for the Banff Film Festival Book Award and was cited as 'the best Dolomite guidebook ever produced' (*SA Mountain Magazine*). James also works as a professional photographer and has won 12 international photography competitions and published work in numerous magazines and papers including *National Geographic*, *The Times* and *The Daily Telegraph*. He has written tutorial and blog posts for a number of popular media platforms such as Viewbug and 500px and appeared as a judge in several global competitions.

Although based in the UK, James spends much of his time exploring the Italian Dolomites and is one of the leading authorities on the region, particularly with regards to photography and extreme sports. He is part of the Norrøna Pro Team and is kindly supported by Breakthrough Photography, Landcruising and Hilleberg.

James can be contacted at www.jamesrushforth.com.

SKI TOURING AND SNOWSHOEING IN THE DOLOMITES

50 WINTER ROUTES

by James Rushforth

2 POLICE SQUARE, MILNTHORPE, CUMBRIA LA7 7PY
www.cicerone.co.uk

© James Rushforth 2017
First edition 2017
ISBN 978 1 85284 745 6

Printed by KHL Printing, Singapore
A catalogue record for this book is available from the British Library.
All photographs are by the author unless otherwise stated.

Route mapping by Lovell Johns www.lovelljohns.com
Overview map by Nicola Regine
Contains OpenStreetMap.org data © OpenStreetMap
contributors, CC-BY-SA. NASA relief data courtesy of ESRI

Updates to this guide

While every effort is made by our authors to ensure the accuracy of guidebooks as they go to print, changes can occur during the lifetime of an edition. Any updates that we know of for this guide will be on the Cicerone website (www.cicerone.co.uk/745/updates), so please check before planning your trip. We also advise that you check information about such things as transport, accommodation and shops locally. Even rights of way can be altered over time.

The route maps in this guide are derived from publicly-available data, databases and crowd-sourced data. As such they have not been through the detailed checking procedures that would generally be applied to a published map from an official mapping agency, although naturally we have reviewed them closely in the light of local knowledge as part of the preparation of this guide.

We are always grateful for information about any discrepancies between a guidebook and the facts on the ground, sent by email to updates@cicerone.co.uk or by post to Cicerone, 2 Police Square, Milnthorpe LA7 7PY, United Kingdom.

Front cover: The north faces of the iconic Tre Cime (Route 49)

CONTENTS

Acknowledgements

The creation of this guidebook was only made possible by the enormous and generous support of a great many people. First and foremost thanks to all the visionaries who came before us, discovering new routes, documenting old ones and developing the area into the hugely successful region we see today. The fine and delicate balance of preserved natural beauty combined with an incredible tourist infrastructure, ultimately resulting in the award of UNESCO world heritage status, is testament to the hard work and dedication of the local populace.

While working on the guide, Collett's Mountain Holidays very kindly provided accommodation in between my stints in the van, a very generous and much appreciated gesture when it's -20°C at night. A huge thanks to the office and resort staff for hosting and for treating me as one of their own.

My thanks to everyone who has accompanied me on countless adventures in the Dolomites, whether on routes included in this guide or not. It has been a true privilege exploring the mountains with you, leaving me with many a cherished memory and ultimately reminding me of what guidebook writing is all about.

As ever my family provided excellent support, guidance and encouragement throughout the project. Thanks as always to Lynne Hempton for accompanying me on many of the routes, for assisting with all aspects of the book and for turning my inarticulate musings into something resembling intelligible text.

Finally my thanks to all the staff at Cicerone who have cajoled, assisted, steered and shaped the evolution of this project from its initial concept to the book you see before you.

Mountain Safety

All mountain activities have their dangers, and those described in this guidebook are no exception. All who ski tour or snowshoe in the mountains should recognise this and take responsibility for themselves and their companions along the way. The author and publisher have made every effort to ensure that the information contained in this guide was correct when it went to press, but they cannot accept responsibility for any loss, injury or inconvenience sustained by any person using this book.

International Distress Signal *(emergency only)*
Six blasts on a whistle (and flashes with a torch after dark) spaced evenly for one minute, followed by a minute's pause. Repeat until an answer is received. The response is three signals per minute followed by a minute's pause.

Helicopter Rescue
The following signals are used to communicate with a helicopter:

Help needed:
raise both arms
above head to
form a 'Y'

Help not needed:
raise one arm
above head, extend
other arm downward

Emergency telephone numbers
If telephoning Italy from the UK the dialling code is: 0039
Carabinieri: ☎ 0165 84 22 25; Emergency Services: ☎ 118

Weather reports
☎ 0165 44 113

Note Mountain rescue can be very expensive – be adequately insured.

Symbols used on route maps

〜	route
⌒ ⌒	alternative route
Ⓢ	start point
Ⓕ	finish point
ⓈⒻ	start/finish point
Ⓢ	alternative start point
Ⓕ	alternative finish point
ⓈⒻ	alternative start/finish point
	glacier
	woodland
	lake
〜	river
━■━	station/railway
╱	cablecar/lift
▲	peak
⬆ ⬆	manned/unmanned refuge
⍍	campsite
■	building
⸸	church or chapel
P	parking
)(	pass
✳	viewpoint
⬆ ⬕ ⍩	hotel/bar/restaurant

Relief
in metres

3200–3400
3000–3200
2800–3000
2600–2800
2400–2600
2200–2400
2000–2200
1800–2000
1600–1800
1400–1600
1200–1400
1000–1200
800–1000
600–800
400–600
200–400
0–200

SCALE: 1:50,000

0 kilometres 0.5   1

0 miles   0.5

Contour lines are
drawn at 25m intervals
and highlighted at
100m intervals.

GPX files

GPX files for all routes can be downloaded for free at www.cicerone.co.uk/745/GPX.

9

Warning

Ski touring, snowshoeing and winter mountaineering can be a dangerous activity carrying a risk of personal injury or death. It should only be undertaken by those with the training and experience to evaluate the routes, a full understanding of the risks, and the appropriate equipment for the chosen route. While every care and effort has been taken in the preparation of this guide, the user should be aware that conditions, especially in winter, are highly variable and can change quickly. Varying snow levels, temperatures, wind conditions and fresh snowfall can seriously affect the character of a route and avalanche risk must be carefully considered. These can materially affect the seriousness of any climb, tour, snowshoe or expedition.

Therefore, except for any liability which cannot be excluded by law, neither Cicerone nor the author accepts liability for damage of any nature (including damage to property, personal injury or death) arising directly or indirectly from the information in this guide.

Route symbols on annotated photo topos

 route line for snowshoeing route in view and ascent for ski touring route in view

 descent for ski touring route in view

 route line for snowshoeing route out of view and ascent for ski touring route out of view

 descent for ski touring route out of view

 route direction

 ski touring route

 snowshoeing route

Passing the impressive icefall in the lower half of Canale Col Anton

ROUTE SUMMARY TABLE

Route	Title	Start/Finish	Distance	Total ascent	Total descent	Grade	Time	SS or ST	Page
Canazei: Val di Fassa									
1	Latemar Labyrinth	Passo Costalunga	10km	150m	150m	E	5–6hrs	SS	45
2	Val San Nicolò	Near Val San Nicolò	16km	600m	600m	E	4–5hrs	SS	49
3	Forcia Neigra	Ciampac cablecar	5km	250m	1060m	F 3.1	2–3hrs	ST	54
4	Val Duron	Campitello/Saltria	14km	765m	500m	E 1.3	5–6hrs	SS&ST	57
5	Forcella Sassolungo Nord	Sasso Levante chairlift/Monte Pana	6km	340m	900m	F 2.2	3–4hrs	ST	62
Canazei and Arabba: Sella Group									
6	Val Mesdì	Pordoi cablecar/Corvara pistes	8km	150m	1500m	F 2.3	2–3hrs	ST	69
7	Canale del Ghiacciaio	Pordoi cablecar/Corvara pistes	9km	400m	1750m	PD 3.2	3–4hrs	ST	74
8	Canale Col Anton into Val Lasties	Pordoi cablecar/Rifugio Pian Schiavaneis	7km	100m	1200m	F 3.3	2–3hrs	ST	78
9	Val Setus	Pordoi cablecar/Corvara pistes	8km	350m	1300m	F 3.3	3–4hrs	ST	82
Ortisei and Selva: Val Gardena									
10	Compaccio	Siusi allo Sciliar lift station	14km	250m	250m	E	4–5hrs	SS	89
11	Alpe di Siusi traverse	Williams Hütte/Saltria	10km	200m	600m	F	4–5hrs	SS	91
12	Chiesetta di San Giacomo and Monte Pic	Sacun	9km	700m	700m	F	5–6hrs	SS	96

Route	Title	Start/Finish	Distance	Total ascent	Total descent	Grade	Time	SS or ST	Page
13	Forcella di Mesdì	Col Riaser gondola/Seceda cablecar	10km	760m	1015m	F 3.1	4–5hrs	ST	99
14	Forcella della Roa	Col Riaser gondola/ Longiarù outskirts	12km	600m	1200m	E 3.1	3–4hrs	ST	105
Corvara: South Badia									
15	Val de Chedul and Col Toronn	Rifugio Jimmy/Vallunga	7km	300m	900m	F 2.2	3–4hrs	ST	111
16	Forcella de Ciampei	Colfosco/Vallunga	8km	450m	750m	F 3.1	3–4hrs	ST	116
17	Pisciadù and the Ciampac traverse	Corvara	12km	350m	700m	E	4–5hrs	SS	119
18	Santa Croce and Ranch da Andrè	Sas dla Crusc chairlift/Badia Abtei	9km	50m	760m	E 1.3	3–4hrs	SS&ST	124
19	Lech dla Lunch to Lech da Sompont	Badia Abtei	7km	225m	225m	E	2–3hrs	SS	128
San Martino in Badia: North Badia and Fanis									
20	Monte Muro	Pe de Börz	13km	650m	650m	E 2.1	5–6hrs	SS&ST	135
21	Crep dales Dodesc	Longiarù outskirts	11km	850m	850m	E 2.2	4–5hrs	ST	139
22	Munt da Medalges	Longiarù outskirts	11km	900m	900m	E 1.3	4–5hrs	SS&ST	143
23	Malga Vaciara	Longiarù	12km	800m	800m	E	5–6hrs	SS	146
24	Utia Lavarella circuit	Pederù	13km	500m	500m	E 1.3	4–5hrs	SS&ST	150
25	Col Becchei Dessora	Pederù	15km	800m	800m	F	4–5hrs	ST	154

Route	Title	Start/Finish	Distance	Total ascent	Total descent	Grade	Time	SS or ST	Page
26	Monte Castello	Pederù	18km	750m	750m	E 2.1	5–6hrs	ST	157
Arabba: Marmolada and Livinallongo									
27	Punta Penia	Rifugio Pian dei Fiacconi/Lago di Fedaia	6km	730m	1300m	PD 3.2	4–5hrs	ST	165
28	Forcella Marmolada	Rifugio Pian dei Fiacconi/Ciampac cablecar parking	11km	300m	1440m	PD 3.1	3–4hrs	ST	169
29	Monte Sief	Corte	8km	750m	750m	E 2.1	4–5hrs	SS&ST	173
San Cassiano: Passo Falzarego									
30	Settsass	Rifugio Valparola	13km	600m	600m	F	5–6hrs	SS	179
31	Forcella Grande	Lagazuoi cablecar/Armentarola	6km	200m	1300m	F 3.2	3–4hrs	ST	183
32	Cadin di Fanis	Lagazuoi cablecar/Passo Falzarego	10km	800m	1600m	F 2.2	5–6hrs	ST	187
33	Canale della Nonna	Passo Falzarego	10km	800m	800m	F 3.2	3–4hrs	ST	191
34	Col dei Bos	Passo Falzarego	10km	800m	800m	F 2.2	5–6hrs	SS&ST	195
35	Cinque Torri and Nuvolau	Rifugio Scoiattoli	8km	350m	725m	E	3–4hrs	SS	199
36	Tofana di Rozes	Rifugio Dibona	10km	1200m	1200m	F 3.3	5–6hrs	ST	203

Route	Title	Start/Finish	Distance	Total ascent	Total descent	Grade	Time	SS or ST	Page
Selva di Cadore: Passo Giau									
37	Monte Pore	Rifugio Fedare/Cernadoi	6km	400m	900m	F 3.3	3–4hrs	SS&ST	209
38	Monte Mondeval	Passo Giau	7km	700m	700m	E 2.1	3–4hrs	ST	213
39	Lastoni di Formin	Passo Giau/Rifugio Malga Pezie de Paru	10km	650m	1200m	F 2.1	4–5hrs	ST	216
40	Croda da Lago	Ponte de Rocurto	11km	900m	900m	F	5–6hrs	SS	221
Pecol: Val di Zoldo									
41	Col de la Puina	Passo Staulanza	6km	650m	650m	F 2.1	3–4hrs	SS&ST	227
42	Città di Fiume	Passo Staulanza	10km	250m	350m	E	4–5hrs	SS	230
43	Rifugio Venezia traverse	Rifugio Palafavera	12km	450m	450m	E	5–6hrs	SS	234
44	Spiz de Zuel	Chiesa outskirts	12km	800m	800m	E	5–6hrs	SS	237
Cortina and Misurina: Passo Tre Croci and Tre Cime									
45	Malga Ra Stua	Sant' Uberto	10km	350m	350m	E	3–4hrs	SS	243
46	Posporcora and Col Rosa circuit	North of Cortina	14km	400m	400m	E	5–6hrs	SS	246
47	Forcella Faloria traverse	Rio Gere/Acquabona	9km	620m	1200m	F 2.2	4–5hrs	ST	250
48	Passo del Cristallo	Passo Tre Croci/Rio Val Fonda parking	9km	1000m	1370m	PD 2.2	5–6hrs	ST	254
49	Giro delle Tre Cime	Lago Antorno	18km	900m	900m	F 2.2	6–7hrs	SS&ST	258
50	Sasso di Sesto	Bad Moos	12km	950m	950m	F 2.3	4–5hrs	SS&ST	262

15

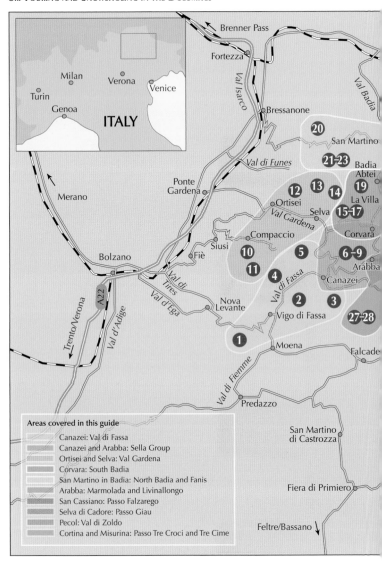

Areas covered in this guide

Canazei: Val di Fassa
Canazei and Arabba: Sella Group
Ortisei and Selva: Val Gardena
Corvara: South Badia
San Martino in Badia: North Badia and Fanis
Arabba: Marmolada and Livinallongo
San Cassiano: Passo Falzarego
Selva di Cadore: Passo Giau
Pecol: Val di Zoldo
Cortina and Misurina: Passo Tre Croci and Tre Cime

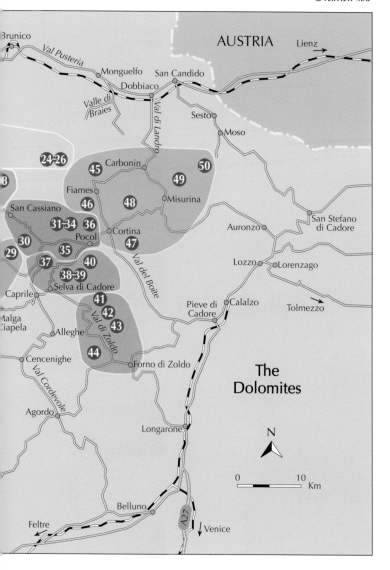

AUSTRIA

Lienz

Brunico

Val Pusteria

Monguelfo

San Candido

Dobbiaco

Valle di Braies

Val di Landro

Sesto

Moso

24-26

Carbonin

45

49

50

Fiames

46

48

Misurina

San Cassiano

8

31-34 **36**

Cortina

47

Auronzo

San Stefano di Cadore

30

Pocol

29

35

37

40

Val del Boite

Lozzo

Lorenzago

38-39

Selva di Cadore

Caprile

41

Pieve di Cadore

Calalzo

Tolmezzo

Malga Ciapela

42

43

Val di Zoldo

Alleghe

Cencenighe

44

Forno di Zoldo

The Dolomites

Val Cordevole

Agordo

Longarone

N

0   10 Km

Belluno

Feltre

A27

↓ Venice

Snowshoes and Monte Pelmo (Route 42)

INTRODUCTION

The Dolomites are an ideal location for a winter holiday

The dramatic spires of the Dolomites, famously described by Reinhold Messner as 'the most beautiful mountain range in the world', are exceptionally popular during the winter months and are home to one of the largest pisted ski areas in the world. The 'Sella Ronda', a circular network of lifts and pistes that can be completed in either direction around the Sella Massif, is particularly popular and draws thousands of visitors every year.

Yet away from the hustle and bustle of the piste lies an intricate network of peaks, ridges, couloirs, open faces and snow-covered valleys; a veritable winter paradise for those willing to venture off the beaten track and explore the backcountry.

The practice of skiing and snowshoeing has had a rather mercurial past. While using skis and snowshoes as a means of transportation over snow is well documented, with snowshoes in particular dating back over 4000 years, their popularity as winter pursuits is only comparatively recent. In the 19th century, as the need to venture into the snowy landscapes for hunting purposes declined, both skis and snowshoes began to be used for enjoyment, particularly in North America and Europe. Then, nearly 100 years later, in 1936 the first chairlift was installed in Idaho, marking a move away from backcountry touring and the beginning of the Alpine ski culture. Recently, as equipment and technologies improve both ski touring and snowshoeing have seen a marked resurgence, and the joy of venturing onto virgin snow is steadily being rediscovered.

From this perspective the Dolomites are the ideal location for a winter holiday as, thanks to the area's popularity as a piste destination, the extensive lift system and excellent road infrastructure provide easy access to some of the most dramatic and inspiring winter locations in the world. The landscape is so unique, the possibilities for exploration so endless and the cultural heritage so diverse that no matter how many times you visit, the Dolomites always have something new to offer: an alternative couloir to ski, a hidden valley to explore, a different dialect to overhear. Those looking to be challenged will rejoice in the steep snowfilled gullies while snowshoers wishing to break fresh trails across deep, untracked snow can delight in the open valleys and hillsides. And, although interest in the backcountry is most certainly on the rise, the wealth of opportunities in the Dolomites combined with the relative unwillingness of many skiers and walkers to venture off the pisted routes means first tracks and untouched expanses of fresh snow can often be found.

Whatever your winter passion, be it technical ski mountaineering, steep couloirs or simply a relaxing snowshoe up a remote snow-covered valley, the Dolomites never fail to delight. This guidebook covers 50 snowshoe and ski touring routes, selected for their beauty, accessibility and the likelihood of favourable winter conditions. As well as some of the classics, included are a few hidden gems that enable you to explore the untouched corners of this magical area, each route focusing on the 'journey' and placing a balanced emphasis on a spectacular and scenically stunning ascent as well as a dramatic and thrilling descent.

HISTORY

The story of the Dolomites began on a coral reef under the waves of the ancient Tethys Ocean some 250 million years ago during the Triassic period. Several million years later in the Eocene period, the African and European plates began to push against one another, causing the uplift and eventual emergence of the Alps, and in turn the Dolomites, from the sea.

It is believed the Dolomites were first inhabited around 8000BC; indeed, the remarkable finding of the Uomo di Mondeval, a perfectly preserved skeleton discovered in 1987 in a burial crypt above San Vito di Cadore, confirmed the passage of Mesolithic hunters nearly 10,000 years ago. The better-known case of Ötzi the Iceman, the mummified corpse of a Copper Age man found in the Otztal Alps in the South Tyrol and now housed in the Archaeology

Museum in Bolzano, is further confirmation of the presence of man in these Alpine areas, although the first stable settlements in the Dolomites were not recorded until 1700BC. It is thought that some of the earliest settlers were people from the Taurisci and Etruscan civilisations, before the colonisation of the Roman Empire a number of centuries later. This brought about significant changes and development to the region, improving the infrastructure of the area and adding transport networks, with concrete findings of Roman houses and roads in the Cadore region dating back to the second century BC. The people in the conquered areas of Northern Italy, parts of Switzerland and Austria shared a common language – a Proto-Indo-European dialect which assimilated parts of the Roman language and was effectively the precursor to Ladin, the dialect spoke in much of the Dolomites today.

As the Roman Empire approached its demise, tribes from the east invaded, destroying much of the Ladin populace. Around AD600, Bavarian tribes began to colonise Northern Italy, bringing a Germanic influence to many of the previously 'Ladin' areas of the Dolomites.

The Middle Ages were characterised by the Christianisation of the former Roman civilisations, and parts of the Dolomites were some of the earliest Venetian and Trentino bishopdoms, then in 1788 the 'Pale Mountains' earned their current denomination, when a French scientist named Dieudonné Sylvain Guy Trancrède Grater de Dolomieu took a rock sample from the Adige valley and sent it off for analysis. The sample, a calcium and magnesium carbonate, was heralded as a new mineral and was given the name of its discoverer, which, in turn, was applied to the mountains themselves. The 18th century saw significant advances in the road and transport infrastructure, allowing explorers, mountaineers and scientists to access the region. It also heralded the start of the region's tourism industry as the first tourists, predominantly upper class Europeans, came to visit the mountains.

However, it was the tragic events that unfolded between 1914 and 1918 that really shaped the cultural legacy of the Dolomites that we see today. After remaining neutral for a long period, Italy declared war on Austro-Hungary in May 1915. Due to bad intelligence, the Italian forces advanced slowly, inadvertently giving the Austrians time to withdraw from the lowlands around Cortina and to fortify their positions in the Sorapis and Cristello ranges. At an impasse, both sides went to ground and a period of intense trench warfare began, with neither side able to make any significant progress.

On 24 October 1917 near the town of Caporetto (modern day Kobarid in Slovenia), the Italian forces suffered one of their greatest defeats in military history. In a move that formed the basis for Ernest Hemingway's *Farewell to Arms*, the combined Austrian and German armies forced the Italians to retreat to the Piave river just east of Venice, ending the so-called 'White War' of the Dolomites.

Physical evidence of the First World War can be seen while undertaking many of the routes in this book, from the commemorative plaques found on Malga Ra Stua (Route 45) where the first fighting began, to the trenches and lookout positions of Cinque Torri (Route 35) and the barbed wire summit of Col dei Bos (Route 34). Col di Lana, the main summit of the neighbouring Monte Sief (Route 29), was dubbed 'Col di Sangue' (blood mountain) by the locals and lost a large section of its summit courtesy of five tonnes of explosive. The ascent in the cablecar to Monte Lagazuoi (Routes 31 and 32) overlooks the lookout windows of the vast network of tunnels within the mountain and the huge explosive crater just southeast of the summit, the result of an Italian attempt to blow up the Austrian position from underneath.

Following the end of hostilities the subsequent 1919 Paris Peace Conference awarded Italy a substantial part of the South Tyrol for its wartime contributions, 90 per cent of which was German speaking. What followed was a systematic and brutal Italianisation program under the Mussolini regime to indoctrinate the Tyrolean people into Italian culture and language. After years of discontent, in 1991 this provoked a mandate from the European Court of Human Rights leading to the completion of 'Il Pachetto' – an agreement to promote the harmonious co-existence of the two cultures. Overall this has been hugely successful and has been hailed as one of the world's greatest examples of the complete integration of an ethnic minority, giving rise to the trilingual and diverse culture enjoyed by the Dolomites today.

LANGUAGE AND CULTURE

Located in northern Italy, the Dolomites offer a unique and exciting blend of Italian and South Tyrolean culture enriched with a strong Austrian influence. Local people place great value in their traditions and many of the most interesting and iconic traits from each of the three cultures have now fused to form part of everyday life.

In testimony to this diverse cultural heritage, today the Dolomites are trilingual, and Italian, German and Ladin are widely spoken throughout the region. The latter, a Romance language with its roots in vernacular Latin, has seen a dramatic resurgence and received official state recognition. Every citizen has the right to speak their own mother tongue and signs often feature all three languages. To make matters even more confusing, places often have three different names: as an example, Canazei, one of the principal towns of the Val di

Approaching the second ascent up to Monte Mondeval with fantastic views of Pelmo (Route 38)

Fassa and a recommended base for this guidebook, is known as 'Canazei' in Italian, 'Kanetschei' in German and 'Cianacèi' in Ladin. For the purposes of this guide, place names will be given in Italian so as to correlate as much as possible with the most widely used maps of the region. A reference table giving the most commonly used Italian and German names for major towns and mountains in the Dolomites is provided in Appendix A. Appendix B offers a list of mountain terms in English, Italian and German.

The Dolomites have a rich heritage of craftsmanship and the local populace is famous for its skill at creating beautiful and original handcrafted ornaments, carvings and sculptures. Often this knowledge is handed down through family generations, although these days the art

of working with iron, brass, timber and glass is also taught at specialist schools such as the Art High School in Cortina. Of these, woodcraft is perhaps the most popular and is particularly prevalent in the Ampezzo basin and Val Gardena, where the numerous woodcarving workshops can be easily identified by the ornate sculptures adorning the exterior.

GETTING THERE

By air

To access the Dolomites by air, the key airports are Venice or Treviso in Italy or Innsbruck in Austria. There are frequent flights from major UK airports throughout the year, although helpfully for this guidebook these tend to be more frequent in the

23

winter. Having touched down, allow for around two and a half hours' driving to reach the villages. All three towns are worthy of a visit in their own right although Venice is particularly recommended, not only because public transport into the centre from both Treviso or Venice Marco Polo airports is exceptionally convenient but also because the city is much quieter in the winter months.

Hiring a car is highly recommended in order to enjoy maximum flexibility once in the Dolomites and to access some of the more remote routes, although there are public transport options from the airports (see Appendix C for the contact details of transfer companies).

In addition to Cortina Express, there are a number of private coach transfer companies which can offer a more expensive but convenient alternative, as well as opening up flight options to more distant airports such as Verona and Munich. Expect to pay something in the region of €70 each way for the transit.

From Treviso or Venice
The Cortina Express transfer service runs twice daily to and from Treviso and Venice airports. Tickets must be booked in advance and the departure times can be difficult to make if arriving on a late flight, but the service is fairly reliable and costs around €30 one way. A more economical but admittedly slightly convoluted option is to take a bus to the train station of either town, a train to Belluno and then use the public bus service towards Agordo and Arabba to reach the Dolomites. This usually works out as the cheapest option but as there are numerous changes and the services

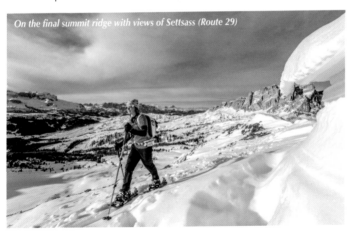

On the final summit ridge with views of Settsass (Route 29)

can be limited, the journey takes considerable planning and can take the best part of a day.

From Innsbruck

To reach the Dolomites from Innsbruck, the best option is to take a bus to the train station and then a train to Ponte Gardena, continuing to the Val Gardena using the public bus service.

By car

If you choose to drive from the UK/ Continental Europe, the quickest route is to take a ferry to Calais or Dunkirk then drive through France, Switzerland, Liechtenstein and Italy. However due to French and Swiss motorway tolls this can soon become an expensive option and it can be worth considering an alternative route through Belgium, Germany and Austria, entering Italy via the Brenner Pass. This usually takes around 15hrs and is best undertaken over two days.

GETTING AROUND

Transport throughout the Dolomites is generally excellent for a mountainous region, with a good range of taxis, buses and friendly outdoor enthusiasts willing to share lifts. Hitching can be a viable option although naturally this is easier for snowshoers as opposed to skiers for logistical reasons! See Appendix C for contact details of transport companies and tourist information centres.

In winter the Passo Fedaia on the Canazei side to the top of the pass is often shut, as is the Passo delle Erbe from the Val di Funes side to the top. Other passes might close during heavy snowfall or in the spring when the temperatures rise. Tourist information offices are the best way of checking if a pass is open.

Lift pass

It is well worth investing in a lift pass to allow a speedy and hassle-free return from linear routes, as well as enabling the combination of some of the interconnected routes into a single excursion. Although some of the main directions are signed, be sure to pick up a piste map from the local ski pass office when planning a return via the lift system.

As a general guide, you can buy either a local pass for a particular valley or a full pass which covers all 450 lifts in the Dolomiti Superski network, including the Sella Ronda. There are numerous options for single and multiday passes, and individual tickets are available for certain lifts. Ski pass information can be found at: www. dolomitisuperski.com/en/ski-pass.

Driving in the Dolomites

If you decide to hire a car, remember to take your driving licence and the card you booked the rental with. As a result of UK legislation, which came into force in 2015 and abolished the paper counterpart, you may also need a licence 'check code' which can be

Approaching the summit of Piz Boè with views over the Marmolada (Route 7)

acquired free of charge from www. gov.uk and is valid for 21 days.

When driving any vehicle in the Dolomites between the months of October and April, whether a hire car or your personal vehicle, it is a legal requirement to either use winter tyres or carry snow chains, although both are recommended. These may not come as part of a standard rental agreement so be sure to check before hiring.

In addition to the winter equipment, reflective jackets, a warning triangle, beam deflectors on right-hand drive vehicles and proof of insurance must also be carried at all times.

WHEN TO GO

The winter season runs from early December to late April and most of the routes in this book should come into condition during that period. However due to seasonable variations it is always worth checking the conditions in advance before planning a trip, particularly at either end of the season. Equally as some of the routes in this book are accessed using the Dolomiti Superski lift system, it is worth considering that the ski lifts usually stop running in early April. As a general indication, conditions tend to improve as the season goes on and the snow base is consolidated, providing a more enjoyable and essentially 'wintery' experience.

ACCOMMODATION

The tourism infrastructure in the Dolomites is exceptionally well developed and all the major towns are liberally provisioned with accommodation options ranging from the basic to the luxurious. Hotels often boast 'wellness' facilities – usually a sauna and steamroom – ski and boot rooms (often with drying facilities) and a bar or restaurant, often with the option of half board. There is also a wide selection of self catering accommodation available, with options and levels of luxury to suit most budgets and tastes.

For the true mountain experience, many of the *rifugios*, literally meaning refuges but in reality usually rather nice restaurants, often offer overnight accommodation. Some are more basic than others, ranging from single or double rooms, bunkrooms or sometimes a combination of the two. Generally a full sleeping bag isn't required as there will be thick blankets and sheets, but a sleeping bag liner is usually expected. There is usually the choice of '*mezza pension*' (half board), usually consisting of a three-course set menu and a continental breakfast, '*con prima colazione*' (bed and breakfast) or '*solo pernottamento*' (just the stay itself). Prices can range anywhere between €18 and €80 a night, depending on the rifugio and the board basis.

During the winter season the majority of rifugios located near the pistes or popular touring routes are open throughout the season. Some of the more remote locations are not open during the winter months but often offer shelter in the form of very basic 'winter rooms'. It is advisable to check with the local tourist information board or Guides' offices whenever embarking on a trip with the intention of staying at a mountain rifugio as facilities, availability and services can vary greatly depending on the area, the hut and the time of year.

Finally there are a number of campsites in the area, which in the winter are generally geared towards camper vans. These offer electric hookups, boot rooms and drying facilities and can cost something in the region of €6–9 per person, €10 per pitch and €4 for electric hookup per day and can vary significantly between low and high season.

In terms of logistical convenience for the routes in this guide, the towns of Arabba, Canazei, Cortina, San Cassiano and Selva di Gardena can be confidently recommended both for their beauty and geographical location. These towns and other suitable locations are covered in more detail in the section introductions below.

The Dolomites are a popular winter destination and accommodation can fill up rather quickly, so consider booking early to avoid disappointment, particularly if intending to travel during peak season. For accommodation options, contact local tourist offices and/or search online. Tourist offices and recommended websites are listed in Appendix C.

FOOD AND DRINK

The area is renowned for its culinary offerings and boasts the highest concentration of Michelin starred restaurants in Italy. A fusion of traditional Italian, Tyrolean and Ladin styles, the cuisine is characterised by its simplicity and yet is full of bold and fresh flavours. Visitors to the region can look forward to traditional Italian pizzas and pasta dishes, Austrian-style dumplings and strudels and Ladin 'Furtaies', a fried dessert typically served with local jam, all in the same restaurant.

To accompany the culinary delicacies, the area also boasts many wine and spirits specialities. There are numerous independent distilleries and most bars will offer a range of locally produced spirits, while the vineyards of the Piana Rotaliana plateau in the outlying Trentino region produce some of the most prized wines in Italy. Grappa, a grape-based pomace brandy first created by Italian wine producers to eek a little extra profit from their grapes, is now a popular spirit throughout the country and will doubtless be encountered in the bars and rifugios dotting the towns and ski slopes.

Italian coffee is justifiably famous and the Dolomites are no exception, offering good coffee in nearly every conceivable form (to score points with the locals, just remember thou shalt only drink cappuccino, caffè latte or any milky coffee in the morning, and never after a meal). For those craving coffee after a meal, 'Caffè Corretto' is a popular option for the brave, an espresso which is 'corrected' with a shot of grappa.

While the après-ski scene in the Dolomites is more low-key than in many of its French counterparts, there is still plenty of fun to be had in the major villages and there are a number of bars and clubs offering great opportunities to enjoy the local nightlife.

TRAVEL AND HEALTH INSURANCE

EHIC scheme

UK citizens currently have reciprocal healthcare rights in Italy thanks to the European Health Insurance Card (EHIC) scheme, formerly known as E111. The card is free of charge for UK citizens and can be applied for online. It is worth carrying this with you at all time as depending on the hospital and type of treatment, simply showing the card may be enough to ensure free treatment, although sometimes you may be required to pay upfront before claiming the costs back through the EHIC system. Private clinics will almost always charge for treatment and this is not always covered under the EHIC scheme.

Most of the towns and villages in the Dolomites have a small health centre which can deal with minor injuries and illness. Some of these have X-ray facilities and will otherwise be able to advise which hospital to go to. These may be the state-governed red cross or the regional white/

Poor visibility and winter conditions can make navigation difficult

green cross variants. There are numerous pharmacies (*farmacia/apotheke*) that can process prescriptions, but most prescribed medicines must be paid for.

Travel insurance

In addition to the EHIC, personal travel insurance is strongly recommended to cover rescue, medical and repatriation costs in the event of an accident. The BMC offer excellent insurance packages: www.thebmc. co.uk/insurance. If you choose to use an alternative insurer, be sure to check that off-piste mountainous activities such as ski touring and snowshoeing are covered as these are usually excluded from standard snowsports packages.

MOUNTAIN SAFETY

Society speaks and all men listen,
mountains speak and
wise men listen. — *John Muir*

In addition to the information contained below, the further reading section in Appendix E has plenty of recommended reading options, including books on how to stay safe in the mountains.

Telephone numbers and apps

If you require the emergency services in the Dolomites, including mountain rescue, dial 118. Mobile phone coverage is generally very good in the region and there are only a few 'black spots' in the more remote areas. If you find yourself in an area with no signal, the official advice from the Italian Mountain Rescue Service is to turn off the mobile phone, turn it back on and instead of inserting the pin code (if you have one), dial the European Emergency Number 112. This will override any network roaming settings and use any available signal.

There are also numerous smartphone apps for emergencies such as 'Echo112', which automatically dials the correct emergency service number while providing your GPS location in a single touch.

Navigation
Navigation is inherently more difficult in the winter as many of the paths and waymarks are hidden from view and visibility is often reduced. The maps

provided in this guide are intended for reference only and should be used in conjunction with a detailed 1:25.000 walking map. The correct Tabacco Map number for each route is given in the information box at the start of each itinerary.

Weather forecasts
For the Dolomites general weather forecast and avalanche forecast, see www.arpa.veneto.it An alternative is to use one of the many weather forecast apps available.

AVALANCHE RISK
There is a common misconception that avalanches are 'acts of God' and that those caught in their path are simply unlucky, citing the old cliché of

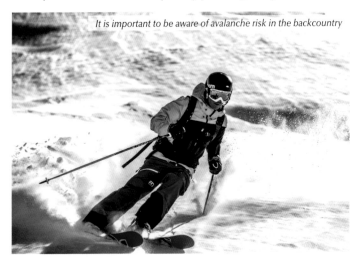
It is important to be aware of avalanche risk in the backcountry

Avalanche danger scale

Avalanche danger is determined by the likelihood, size and distribution of avalanches.

Danger level	Travel advice	Likelihood of avalanches	Avalanche size and distribution
5 Extreme	Avoid all avalanche terrain.	Natural and human triggered avalanches certain.	Large to very large avalanches in many areas.
4 High	Very dangerous avalanche conditions. Travel in avalanche terrain not recommended.	Natural avalanches likely; human triggered avalanches very likely.	Large avalanches in many areas; or very large avalanches in specific areas.
3 Considerable	Dangerous avalanche conditions. Careful snowpack evaluation, cautious route finding and conservative decision making essential.	Natural avalanches possible; human triggered avalanches likely.	Small avalanches in many areas; or large avalanches in specific areas; or very large avalanches in isolated areas.
2 Moderate	Heightened avalanche on specific terrain features. Evaluate snow and terrain carefully; identify features of concern.	Natural avalanches unlikely; human triggered avalanches possible.	Small avalanches in specific areas; or large avalanches in isolated areas.
1 Low	Generally safe avalanche conditions. Watch for unstable snow on isolated terrain features.	Natural and human triggered avalanches unlikely.	Small avalanches in isolated areas or extreme terrain.

Safe backcountry travel requires training and experience. You control your own risk by choosing where, when and how you travel.

being in the wrong place at the wrong time. In reality, between 80 to 90 per cent of avalanches are load-triggered or, in layman's terms, caused by the weight of skiers or snowshoers travelling through the backcountry.

Only one in two people buried above the head survive an avalanche, with death most commonly attributed to asphyxiation but also as a result of injuries sustained during the initial movement of snow. As a result, prevention is almost certainly better than cure and it is fundamental to have a good knowledge of snowpack and snow conditions before attempting any of the routes in this guide.

Avalanche courses are readily available throughout the Alpine areas of Europe, while in the UK both Plas y Brenin in North Wales and Glenmore Lodge in Scotland offer excellent multi-day training programmes.

Avalanche theory

Remember that avalanches generally occur on slopes that are 30 degrees or greater. By avoiding unnecessary traversing on and under steeper slopes the risk of being caught is greatly reduced.

Check the avalanche forecast but don't take the warning level as gospel; most fatalities occur when the international avalanche danger scale is at 3 – considerable. Conditions should always be continually evaluated throughout the duration of a route.

Heavy snow falling at over one inch per hour greatly increases the danger of an unstable snowpack due to the additional weight loading and because the fresh snow has insufficient time to bond to underlying snow layers.

Strong winds are particularly dangerous as they move snow from windward to leeward slopes often far more quickly than heavy snowfall. This results in poorly bonded 'wind-slab' layers on leeward slopes, which

are especially susceptible to weight loading.

A sudden rise in temperature, rain or spring conditions can affect different layers of the snowpack and lubricate already weak layers, often resulting in large slides. This is particularly true of south and west facing slopes during the spring when an early start following a cold night is essential.

Be careful not to place too much faith in trees. While trees do provide snowpack stability they only do so if they are very closely spaced and afford no extra protection on open slopes.

Reducing risk

- Try to avoid travelling alone: two is better and three better still
- Ensure a safe distance is kept between party members
- Never traverse above a member of your party or anyone else in a risk-prone area
- When crossing a dangerous slope is unavoidable, do so one at a time
- Always try to travel from an area of increased safety to an area of increased safety
- Where possible, be careful of natural terrain traps which are difficult to escape

Be on the lookout for the following 'red flag' indicators

- New snow within 24hrs
- The top layer of snow sliding away on traverses

- Cracking of the snow in front of you
- Whooshing sounds as the air beneath a poorly bonded layer is forced out
- Evidence of previous avalanches indicating that the area is unstable
- Running water underneath the snow
- The occurrence of natural avalanches
- Rapid rises in temperature

If you do get caught in an avalanche

- Try to stay on your feet and cut diagonally sideways to escape to the sides
- Drop your poles and try to release your skis (it is better to avoid locking out the front pins of tech bindings in dangerous terrain where possible)
- Trigger an Avalanche Airbag System pack if you have one
- Adopt a breaststroke/rolling motion to try to stay on top of the slide
- If you're near the surface, stick an arm towards the top to help orientate yourself and to help rescuers locate you
- Adopt a foetal position with your arm in front of your face to create an air pocket just before everything stops moving

When out on route, it is important to constantly monitor the weather and conditions

- Try to remain as calm as possible, breathing slowly
- If the snowpack is sufficiently loose and you're near the surface, carefully try to dig yourself out

If you witness an avalanche

Watch any victims carefully; if there are multiple victims and multiple spotters call out who you're watching. Mark the direction of their resting position with a ski pole. Be careful to mentally mark any larger features (large blocks of snow and debris etc) in relation to the victims' location. This will greatly speed up the search.

Searching after an avalanche

- Stay calm
- Appoint a nominal leader to coordinate the search, allocating searchers/someone to call the emergency services
- Assess the whole situation, taking the safety of the rest of the party into consideration
- Carry out a controlled search pattern based on the facts, considering the number of people in the party, number of victims, type of terrain and positions last seen with particular emphasis on the 'sweet zone' (a 60 degree arc from where the victim was last seen). Use the equipment available to you but do not underestimate sight and sound
- Act as quickly as possible: time is crucial

The key to preventing an avalanche lies in the ability to interpret the conditions and be subsequently fluid with decision making, always accepting that retreat may be necessary.

Checklists for staying safe

Pre-departure

- Check the weather forecast is suitable
- Check the snow conditions and avalanche risk are suitable
- Ensure you have the correct equipment and that all equipment is in good repair
- Read the route description carefully
- Ensure each member of the party has the relevant experience for the chosen itinerary

During the route

- Ensure transceivers are switched on before departing
- Evaluate the snowpack throughout the route
- Keep a safe distance between party members in the event of an avalanche
- Keep all members of the group in sight
- Evaluate the weather throughout the route
- Be careful to choose the safest ascent and descent route depending on the current snow conditions (this may differ to the descent route given in the guidebook)

EQUIPMENT

General equipment for both skiers and snowshoers

Self-rescue kit

A transceiver, shovel and probe are essential items that should be carried when attempting all of the itineraries within this book. It is fundamentally important that all members of the party are familiar with the correct use of all three of these items. Large metal shovels that don't flex in icy snow are preferable.

Eye protection

Snow blindness is very common during the winter even on overcast days. Sunglasses are adequate for most situations although goggles can provide improved visibility in flat light, strong wind or snow.

Walking/skiing poles

Poles greatly assist with balance in winter conditions. Fixed-length or two-piece poles generally offer the best performance in terms of durability and reliability, and large baskets improve efficiency when moving through deep snow.

Avalanche airbag rucksack

As the name suggests, avalanche airbag rucksacks contain one (or sometimes two) large airbags which are inflated by pulling a ripcord attached to your bag in the event of an avalanche. The increased area helps to keep you buoyant and nearer the surface of a slide while also providing a small amount of physical protection during an avalanche. Research conducted by the Swiss Avalanche Institute has suggested that avalanche victims are eight times more likely to survive with a correctly activated airbag than without.

Counter arguments for airbag rucksacks often quote a false sense of security, increased weight and expense as reasons for not taking one. Whatever you decide, it's imperative to remember that prevention is better than cure, and equipment is no substitute for experience and careful planning.

Other equipment

Rucksack, additional layers, a spare pair of gloves, compass, a small first aid kit, food, water, mobile phone (preferably with GPS), hat and map.

Ski touring equipment

Skis

These now come in a huge array of shapes and sizes and the choice can be a little overwhelming when starting out. As a guide, aim to find a balance between size, weight and performance. Longer and wider skis will usually provide better float in deep powder but are heavier and more difficult to manoeuvre when making kick-turns on steep terrain, while shorter and lighter skis might be a dream on the ascent but can be harder

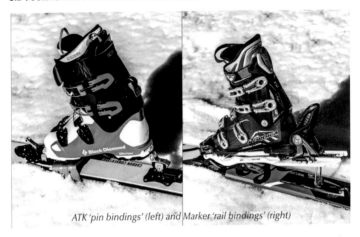

ATK 'pin bindings' (left) and Marker 'rail bindings' (right)

to ski on the way down. 'Touring' skis are generally preferable to 'freeride' skis for the majority of routes within this guide.

Bindings

There are an increasing number of touring bindings on the market. These all differ slightly but essentially fall into two categories: frame bindings and 'AT' (alpine touring) or 'tech' bindings. Frame bindings such as the Marker Royal Family series are compatible with standard downhill boots and work in much the same way as a standard 'alpine' step-in binding, the key difference being the facility to unlock the frame to enable the foot to hinge off the ski. These bindings offer excellent performance on the descent and provide a higher degree of safety due to their DIN-certified release system. Unfortunately this comes at the expense of uphill efficiency as given the weight, picking up the whole binding on each step is extremely tiring and as such frame bindings are generally more suited to 'freeride' descents.

The second type of binding is the Dynafit style 'AT' (alpine touring) binding, also referred to as 'pin' or 'tech' bindings. These feature two points that connect to the front of the ski boot, allowing the toe of the boot to pivot. They are much more efficient on the ascent but only a handful of models are DIN-certified.

Boots

Once again there is a vast range of touring boots on the market. Lightweight boots are ideal but comfort should be the main priority when choosing a pair.

Skins

These need to be cut to the correct size for your skis and checked periodically to ensure they are suitably adhesive. For springtime touring it can be worth rubbing wax into the fibres to prevent the build-up of wet snow.

Ski crampons

A much underrated bit of kit, ski crampons are well worth carrying if you're likely to encounter icy snow or make any exposed traverses.

Helmet

A matter of personal preference, helmets are becoming increasingly popular both on and off piste and modern models are lightweight and comfortable.

Snowshoe equipment

Snowshoes

Much like skis, snowshoes come in a variety of shapes and sizes. The size, traction on the bottom and binding type depends largely on personal preference and your intended usage.

Boots

B1 or B2 walking boots will work well with most snowshoe models; again, comfort and personal preference are the most important factors here.

Additional equipment

More specialised equipment may be required on certain routes and will be specified in the route description.

Crampons

Crampons should be fitted to ski/winter boots as required.

Rope

A single 30-metre rope can often be useful for moving over steep terrain or negotiating cornices at couloir entrances.

Mountaineering kit

Harness, belay devices, slings, rock protection and ice screws.

Walking axe

Size is dependent on personal preference, although a shorter axe is often easier to carry when ski touring. It is important to be familiar with self-arrest techniques on steep terrain.

GRADING

Before embarking on an itinerary it is important to evaluate the technical difficulties of the ascent and descent, taking into account the experience of each member of the party. Snowshoe difficulty is graded using the alpine system, whereas ski tours use a dual grading system that combines the alpine grade for the ascent and the Volo/Toponeige grade for the descent.

It is important to note that both grading systems are extremely subjective and will vary considerably depending on the conditions encountered on the route. A ski descent in perfect condition can feel several

Select routes that suit your ability and level of experience

grades easier, whereas the opposite is true when a route is in poor condition. Unfortunately there is no substitute for experience and if in doubt it is always best to start on easier grades.

Experienced walkers with a good knowledge of mountainous terrain will find any of the snowshoes graded E (Excursion) accessible for a first trip. Advanced piste skiers with some off-piste experience will be able to attempt routes of up to 2.2 providing they are in good condition. However, it is important to note that all of the routes in this book require a good knowledge of backcountry snowpack and winter conditions.

As an example, Route 28 Forcella Marmolada has a difficulty of PD 3.1. The PD grade suggests that some moderate alpinism will be required: in this case the final ascent to Forcella Marmolada itself is steep and often requires crampons, while the subsequent abseil onto the south side requires mountaineering experience. The 3.1 refers to the descent couloir which is initially narrow and steep (40°) before the technical difficulties ease in the lower section through the Val Contrin.

Alpine grade (snowshoe routes and ski ascent)

Snowshoe routes and the ski tour ascents are given an alpine grade, as below.

Alpine grade	Difficulties
E – Excursion	Excursion – Easy terrain in all snow conditions.
F – Facile	Easy alpinism – Easy terrain but in a more alpine and remote environment.
PD – Peu Difficile	Moderate alpinism – Steeper slopes up to 40° with more technical sections on ice and rock often requiring the use of crampons and an ice axe.
AD – Assez Difficile	Quite difficult alpinism – Increasingly steeper slopes with snow and ice up to 50° presenting alpine difficulties.

Volo/Toponeige grade (ski descent)

This scale is fast becoming the go-to grading system for evaluating ski descent difficulties in the Alps. The grades run from 1 to 5 with three decimal points in each category; the higher the number the more difficult it is. The only exception is the grade 5, which is currently open-ended.

Volo/Toponeige grade	Difficulties
Ski 1 (1.1-1.3)	30° or less – Easy and non-technical terrain with wide slopes.
Ski 2 (2.1-2.3)	35° or less – Slopes are steeper and less uniform with occasional technical difficulties.
Ski 3 (3.1-3.3)	35° with sections of 40°/45° – Technical terrain with couloirs and narrow passages.
Ski 4 (4.1-4.3)	40° with sections of 45°/50° – Steep skiing on sustained technical ground with exposed sections.
Ski 5 (5.1 and above)	45° with sections of 50°/55° – Extremely difficult and sustained itineraries on technical ground.

GUIDING SERVICES

Hiring a guide can be a useful option for those wanting extra security on a route or simply to be shown the areas with the best snow and conditions. There are mountain guide offices in all of the major villages, all offering tailored itineraries to suit specific requirements and a set weekly programme featuring some of the most popular itineraries in the Dolomites.

The weekly programmes often have a minimum (and maximum) group number, although all the

OTHER ACTIVITIES IN THE DOLOMITES

With 1200km of piste and 450 lifts covered by a single pass, the Dolomites offer one of the largest pisted ski areas in the world. The ski areas are all incredibly well linked and enable you to cover huge distances, with a number of dedicated on-piste circuits providing easily-navigated routes through the different valleys and regions. The most popular of these is undoubtedly the world famous Sella Ronda, a circuit around the Sella massif which can be completed in either direction. As each ski area features a variety of different pistes ranging from blue to black, as well as dedicated nursery slopes for beginners, there is something to suit every skiing ability.

The lift network also provides access to a number of pisted toboggan slopes which are great fun and highly recommended, particularly for families with children. Sledges can be hired for a small cost from many of the ski hire shops. To experience some toboggan culture, consider a spot of 'Moon Sledding', a South Tyrolean tradition where families enjoy a meal out on the mountain followed by a toboggan back down, traditionally under a full moon.

Cross country or Nordic skiing is also hugely popular in the Dolomites, with over 1000km of pisted tracks throughout the area offering dedicated circuits of varying difficulty. Biathlon shooting ranges are available at some of the larger facilities for those wanting to try the full experience under the watchful eye of an instructor.

The Dolomites also boast some spectacular winter climbing, with countless ice and mixed routes offering superb climbing opportunities for those with the relevant experience. The ice conditions in the Dolomites are reliable and the routes range from short single-pitch routes to extensive multi-pistes, usually surrounded by truly stunning scenery. Serrai di Sottoguda below the Marmolada is the venue of choice for most visitors as it offers a huge variety of falls in a small and easily accessible area. The north faces of the Sella above the town of Colfosco also have a number of superb climbs, the classic 'La Spada di Damocles' attracting winter climbers from far and wide. The superbly situated and dramatic Vallunga branching of Selva di Val Gardena and Val Travenanzes near Cortina both have a number of more remote climbs; these are generally accessed on skis and offer something a little more off the beaten track. The guidebook *Ghiaccio Verticale* published by Idea Montagna covers many of the winter climbing routes in the area, although currently this is only available in Italian.

There are iceskating rinks in Corvara, Arabba, Cortina and most of the larger towns, while curling can be tried at many of the frozen outdoor lakes such as Lago Sompunt and Lago di Braies.

Although paragliding isn't as prevalent during the winter as in the summer it is still possible to book tandem trips from most of the major towns, allowing you to view this unique landscape from a different and unusual perspective. Just be sure to wrap up warm!

If the weather isn't ideal or if you fancy a break from the mountains, the nearby city of Bolzano is well worth a visit. As well as offering plenty of opportunities for retail therapy and a chance to indulge in some of northern Italy's thriving café culture, the town also has a rich architectural heritage, the impressive Gothic cathedral in the main square being of particular note. There are also a number of excellent museums, although the highlight is undoubtedly the South Tyrol Museum of Archaeology, home to a number of excellent historical exhibitions and, most notably, Ötzi the Iceman, Europe's oldest known natural human mummy dating back to 3300BC.

options can be privately booked by individuals at a higher cost. Prices range from €90–350 per day, depending on the itinerary and the group number. All of the mountain guide offices can arrange for English-speaking guides on request, and more information can be found at the websites listed in Appendix D. The offices are also excellent places to get more information about itineraries and to find out the latest snow conditions and avalanche danger.

USING THIS GUIDE

There are 50 ski touring and snow-shoeing itineraries described in this guide. While most of the routes can be attempted on either skis or showshoes, due to the nature of the terrain 36 are best suited to ski touring while 28 are more appropriate as snowshoe routes, naturally with some crossover on itineraries which are equally good on both skis and snow-shoes. Routes are marked with a ski touring or snowshoeing icon (or both), as a guide.

ski touring   snowshoeing

Route descriptions were accurate at the time of writing and are accompanied by an information box stating the start and finish points (as well as the altitude of each), the route length and time without stops, the grading of the route, the cumulative ascent and descent, the aspect of the ascent and descent, and the GPS coordinates of the recommended parking location. An additional section, 'Other possibilities', is included to highlight any possible alternatives and extensions that may be of interest (with the grade provided in brackets). For linear routes, transport information for returning to the start point is also given. Be aware that at busy times of the year, when pistes are crowded and lift queues long, it can take twice as long to get back, so allow plenty of time for the return. Place names on the maps that are significant for route navigation are shown in **bold** in the text.

Each route is complemented by a 1:50,000 overview map extract which is intended for use in conjunction with a 1:25,000 Italian Tabacco map; the correct map number is provided in the information box at the beginning of each route. Additionally, where possible, an annotated photo topo has been included to show the entire route or a section of the route which is particularly difficult to navigate. On the ski tours the ascent is denoted in red route lines and blue route lines show the descent; on the snowshoe routes the whole line is denoted in red. GPX files for all routes can be downloaded for free at www.cicerone. co.uk/745/GPX.

For the purposes of this guidebook, the most popular areas of the central and northern Dolomites are included; the Pala group located to the south and the Brenta group to the west are not included due to their more remote and outlying locations.

CANAZEI: VAL DI FASSA

Leaving one of the Labyrinth tunnels (Route 1)

INTRODUCTION

The Val di Fassa is one of the principal valleys in the Dolomites and runs roughly southwest to northeast from Moena to Alba di Fassa. The main tourist destination is Canazei, a popular ski village on the southwest corner of the famous Sella Ronda ski route, an immensely popular 44km network of pistes around the imposing Sella massif. A haven for walking and climbing in the summer, in the winter the pretty valleys and dramatic gullies are transformed by crisp white snow, contrasting beautifully with the blue skies and reddish hue of the steep Dolomite rockfaces. A number of smaller valleys branch off the Val di Fassa, the gentle slopes of the Val San Nicolò and the Val Duron providing superb snowshoe and winter walking possibilities.

The Sassolungo group forms the natural border between the Val di Fassa and the Val Gardena and is composed of a number of peaks, namely Punta Grohmann, Torre Innerkofler, Dente, Sassopiatto, the Cinque Dita (meaning five fingers, a nod to the palm-shaped profile when viewed from the northeast) and finally the summit of Sassolungo itself. The ski tour through the centre is a classic itinerary, characterised by a short but steep ascent to Forcella Sassolungo and a varied descent down between the dramatic rock walls to rejoin conveniently with the ski lifts in the Alpe di Siusi area.

The Val di Fassa is probably one of the most developed tourist destinations in the Dolomites and as such boasts a huge array of accommodation options and amenities. Canazei is the obvious option, located at the base of the Pordoi, Sella and Fedaia Passes and so offering excellent access to many of the other areas in this guide. In addition to Canazei, Campitello and Alba also benefit from direct access to the Sella Ronda lift system, while Pozza, Pera and Vigo di Fassa are all well linked by secondary ski areas and ski buses.

ROUTE 1
Latemar Labyrinth

Start/Finish	Hotel Savoy, Passo Costalunga (1745m)
Distance	10km
Total ascent	150m
Total descent	150m
Grade	E
Time	5–6hrs
Aspect of ascent	N
Aspect of descent	N
Map	Tabacco No 06
Parking	Car park at top of Passo Costalunga: 46.40413, 11.6093

This excellent snowshoe traverses under the Latemar peaks, a seldom frequented but beautiful area of the Dolomites which is best known during the summer months for providing the backdrop to the stunning Lago di Carezza. The first 20mins of this route follows the Carezza ski pistes. However, once immersed in the stunning 'Labyrinth' boulderfield beneath the imposing Bambole di Latemar, the 'Latemar dolls', this slightly arduous start to the day will be long forgotten.

APPROACH

From Canazei take the SS48 west for 12km until reaching the town of Vigo di Fassa. Here turn right onto the SS241, following signs for Passo Costalunga/ Passo Carezza. Follow the road uphill for 9km to reach the top of the pass and park adjacent to Hotel Savoy in the lift station parking area.

Begin the walk opposite **Hotel Savoy** and head south, ascending on the right-hand side of the ski pistes and following a small pisted track for 5mins. Turn right to follow the ski piste, which branches off through the woods, keeping to the right side of the piste and being wary of descending skiers. After 15mins it leads out of the trees into an open area where the piste makes a sharp bend to the left. Leave the piste here and continue straight on, joining a pisted track to follow the top of a hilly rise to a cross just below the crest of the hill. There are now stunning views all around, encompassing the Catinaccio, Roda da Vael and the Bambole di Latemar.

At the top of the hill a signpost points to path 13 leading down and right and path 17 continuing straight on. Ignore both of these and keep left, following path 18A towards Cima Latemar. Traverse the slope along path 18A and round a corner to enter an obvious valley characterised by a couloir high on the left. Continue on path 18A, following it around to the right and down the valley, descending through the trees before exiting in a clearing marked by a series of cliffs on the right and the characteristic boulderfield of the Labyrinth straight ahead. Continue towards the boulders to reach a junction with path 18 descending to the right. Stay left here, joining path 20 and entering into the **Labyrinth**.

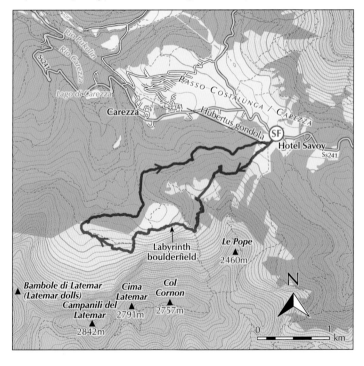

The **Labyrinth boulderfield** was the inspiration for the underground lair in Agatha Christie's Hercule Poirot novel *The Big Four* after her stay at Grand Hotel Carezza in 1926, and so followed the naming of the footpath, Sentiero Agatha Christie.

The path weaves its way through the maze, marked by a single red stripe on the rocks, taking a route that can be hard to follow without tracks. There are some tight squeezes through some of the boulders and caves. In deep snow or when carrying a large rucksack the tight squeezes may be difficult to negotiate and sometimes involve a little circumnavigation! After half an hour in the boulderfield, the route begins to ascend more steeply uphill before traversing out along path 20. It is useful to note that although well marked with red stripes, this is the first time that the number 20 is actually marked.

Traverse for 10mins through a clearing and then into dense trees, exiting into the open again to reach a junction with a path leading right. If time is short this can be used to shortcut the descent but otherwise continue along the main track. This traverses and descends gently into dense woodland, following the natural lie of the land until a junction signing path 11/21 to the pass and Lago di Carezza.

Making ground on the initial part of the route with views of the Latemar group

THE BAMBOLE DI LATEMAR

Local folklore recounts that once upon a time, a group of children were playing near to Lago di Carezza and came across a man who had lost a precious knife. They helped him search but alas the knife could not be found. Sunset came and the children bade the man goodnight and set off to their homes in the village. On the way, one of the children, Minega, saw the knife gleaming in the grass. She picked it up and ran back to the old man, who was delighted and promised her that as a reward he would grant her a wish. The little girl was shy but eventually asked for a doll. As it was already getting dark, the man said if she returned the next day he would let her choose a beautiful doll from his collection. On the way home, Minega met an old woman. How lucky you are, she said, as the old man is rich and owns a great many dolls. Some of his dolls wear silken dresses, but the best ones are clothed in brocade and expensive jewels. If the dolls he gives you wear silk, you must say 'Dolls of stone with silken rags, stay there and look at the Latemar' and he will give you the precious dolls. The next day Minega met the old man, who presented her with a collection of beautiful dolls in gold and red silk dresses. Minega recited the words the old woman had told her, and all of a sudden the air was filled by the cackling laughter of the witch and the dolls turned to stone, creating the red and golden spires of the Latemar peaks.

Continue for 100 metres to another junction where path 11 leads left to the lake.

Apart from in winter, when it freezes entirely, **Lago di Carezza** is well worth a detour. It is beautiful in summer, but at either end of the winter or even during a mild winter, when the banks and trees are sprinkled with snow and only the edges of the lake hold a little ice, it is an idyllic spot.

Continue right onto Sentiero Agatha Christie to yet another sign in 15 metres. Keep left on path 21 here, skirting left around a hill and ascending at a gentle gradient. Another junction, this time with path 13, is reached in 20mins; keep straight on following path 21 towards the Costalunga Pass. The gondola at the start of the route is reached in another 15mins; from here turn left to return easily back to the road.

ROUTE 2
Val San Nicolò

Start/Finish	Ristorante Soldanella (1435m)
Distance	16km
Total ascent	600m
Total descent	600m
Grade	E
Time	4–5hrs
Aspect of ascent	W
Aspect of descent	W
Map	Tabacco No 06
Parking	Opposite Ristorante Soldanella: 46.42041, 11.7061

The Val San Nicolò is an idyllic steep-sided valley, which branches east off the Val di Fassa, carving its way towards Col Ombert and the Marmolada. The gentle incline of the valley floor lends itself perfectly to easy snowshoeing in a dramatic and striking environment, making it an exceptionally popular venue throughout the winter months.

APPROACH

From Canazei follow the SS48 south for just under 10km until reaching a roundabout on the main road on the outskirts of Pozza di Fassa. Turn left, following signposts for the town centre and the Val San Nicolò. Drive through the centre and out of the opposite side of the village for 2km until crossing a bridge over the river with Ristorante Soldanella on the left. Park opposite the restaurant in the roadside parking area.

Cross back over the bridge and immediately turn left onto a wide track which runs along the right-hand side of the river, following this for 15mins until the path descends to join up with the ski piste descending from Rifugio Buffaure. A pisted path to the right of the ski slope continues uphill past **Malga Crocifisso** to reach a junction. Turn left and follow signs for the 'Val San Nicolò' staying on the right-hand side of the ski piste by crossing a small wooden bridge. Shortly after entering the woods, leave the ski piste and continue ascending the large track, first on the right-hand side of the stream and then crossing over onto the left. Some 40mins after passing Malga Crocifisso, the track enters the Val San Nicolò proper, where the summer car park is signed on the right.

Continue straight ahead, staying on the main path and passing many idyllic wooden huts that used to be used by local farmers working in the area. Over to the left, two **Maerins** (rock towers) are visible.

According to local folklore these **pinnacles** are in fact two stone giants standing guard over the valley. The legend goes that Princess Similuce bribed her way past them during her flight from the 'Rosengarten' by giving them each a precious stone. Today the towers host a number of excellent climbing routes, which the locals have very successfully kept hidden from the world's climbing media.

Follow the main path for 20mins, ignoring several turn offs to the right, until reaching the superbly situated **Baita Ciampi**, open during peak season and providing a great spot for a drink. After a pleasant pause here, continue past the rifugio on the main track for a further 15mins to reach a signposted junction where path 641 leads off to the right. From here it is possible to continue up the valley to reach Baita alle Cascate. From here, turn right and follow signs for Forcella del Pief on a smaller path which can be difficult to navigate if it's untracked – keep an eye out for the path markers sparsely painted on the trees. The path heads

southeast, first on the left-hand side of the stream before crossing to the right via a small wooden bridge. This leads to a signpost at **Strada di Rusci** (1896m). From here a possible extension continues straight ahead on path 641 up to Forcella del Pief (see Other possibilities). Turn right and follow another large track which descends the left-hand side of the stream for 40mins, ignoring several turn offs to the left and the right until the track bends to the left and begins to ascend steeply.

51

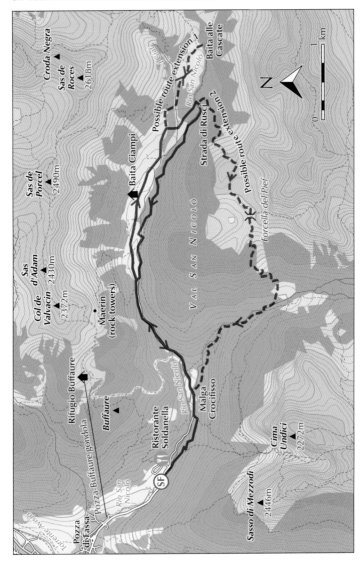

A group approaches the head of the Val San Nicolò

Turn right here to join back onto the main track first ascended at the bottom of the Val San Nicolò. Reverse the approach route to return to the car park in 40mins.

Other possibilities

To extend the snowshoe it is possible to continue up the main valley track to **Baita alle Cascate** at the head of the valley before returning to the turn off onto path 641 to complete the circle (1hr there and back).

If the conditions are safe and the party is suitably experienced the walk can be extended by continuing along path 641 to **Forcella del Pief**, taking in some spectacular views over the valley. The path then descends to follow the bottom of the Valle dei Monzoni back to **Malga Crocifisso**. This extension requires an absolutely safe snowpack and good navigational skills as the path is rarely tracked. (Allow an additional two hours.)

ROUTE 3
Forcia Neigra

Start	Forcia Neigra button lift top station (2300m)
Finish	Ciampac cablecar (1490m)
Distance	5km
Total ascent	250m
Total descent	1060m
Grade	F 3.1
Time	2–3hrs
Aspect of ascent	S
Aspect of descent	E
Map	Tabacco No 06
Parking	Ciampac cablecar car park: 46.45785, 11.78855

This is a lovely circular route around Monte Colac, a beautifully formed mountain at the head of the Val di Fassa, just west of the Marmolada. The ascent up the sunny south side is beautiful and relatively short thanks to the Ciampac lift system, while the descent down a series of open east facing couloirs often offers superb snow with magnificent views over Gran Vernel and the Marmolada range. This itinerary requires a safe snowpack and should not be underestimated as the skiing is technical and the route finding not always obvious, particularly towards the wooded area at the end of the route.

APPROACH

From Canazei follow the SP641 southeast for 3.5km to reach the Ciampac cablecar on the right between the villages of Alba and Penia. Park in the large parking area adjacent to the cablecar station (€5 for the day). Take the cablecar and Sela Brunech chairlift as far as the mid station. Ski down and take the button lift up into the bowl beneath the saddle.

From the top of the button lift, Forcia Neigra is clearly visible to the east: with good eyesight it is even possible to make out the summer signpost at the saddle.

Put skins on and cross through the nearby boulderfield to reach a large buttress. The summer path skirts to the left but in the winter it is often easier to take a direct line with a series of kick turns up to **Forcia Neigra** and the prominent summer signpost (1hr).

From the saddle descend directly below the signpost down a rightwards slanting open couloir. The snow is often a little wind slabbed at the entrance but generally improves lower down where the slope widens. A narrow section funnels

Approaching Forcia Neigra

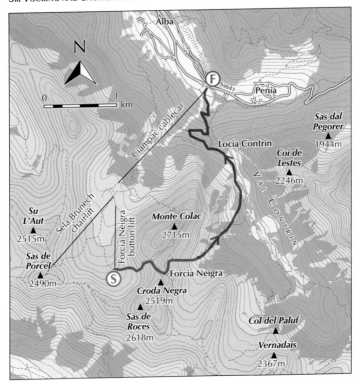

into another open couloir joining from the left. Follow this passing some large boulders creating several narrow passages until reaching a more open area with sparse trees. Navigation can be difficult here – stick high on the left, contouring under the rock walls of Monte Colac and staying above a series of small rocky cliffs until picking up the red and white flags denoting the summer path. Follow this down through denser trees to reach the gentle gradient of the Contrin valley, turning left to follow the bottom of the valley. Some poling leads through a gate to arrive shortly after at the small **Locia Contrin** building. From here follow the large track down a number of hairpins (beware of people touring up) all the way back to the **Ciampac cablecar** parking area. If the snow coverage on the track isn't sufficient to make a ski descent, it is possible to traverse west through the trees to join the piste leading back to the lifts.

ROUTE 4
Val Duron

Start	Campitello (1435m)
Finish	Saltria (1700m)
Distance	14km
Total ascent	765m
Total descent	500m
Grade	E 1.3
Time	5–6hrs
Aspect of ascent	E
Aspect of descent	N
Map	Tabacco No 05
Return to start	Skiers with a lift pass can return to the start using the Dolomiti Superski lift network (allow 2hrs): from Saltria, take the ski bus to Monte Pana then the Monte Seura chairlift back towards the Sella Ronda. Descend the short blue run ahead then take the Tramans chairlift. From here rejoin the Sella Ronda circuit and follow this anti-clockwise to reach Col Rodella. Descend in the Campitello cablecar to return to the centre of the town. A 15mins' walk then leads back to the start. For snowshoers a vehicle drop is recommended as return by public transport is impractical and often impossible. Alternatively, convert the route into an out-and-back itinerary, ascending the valley to Passo Duron before turning around to retrace the route.
Parking	Outskirts of Campitello: 46.47807, 11.74087

This is a long linear route through the Val Duron, an idyllic valley carving west between the Catinaccio group and the vast alpine plateau of the Alpe di Siusi. The route finishes a long way from the start point and a car drop is recommended, leaving a car at Monte Pana and driving the Val Gardena and Passo Sella to the start point in Campitello. The route is also well suited to ski touring as the return is possible using the lift system back to Campitello.

APPROACH

Although the route starts in Campitello, it requires leaving a car at Monte Pana in the Val Gardena. To do this, drive to Santa Cristina, a village located halfway between Ortisei to the west and Selva to the east along the SS242. On entering the village, Monte Pana is well signposted along a very steep and narrow road; snowchains may be required if there is snow on the road. (See map in Route 5 for location of Monte Pana.) Leave a car in one of the many car parks at the top of the road then descend the road in the second car to return to the valley. Turn right and follow the SS242 through Selva to Plan de Gralba, then at the junction for the Sella and Passo Gardenaes continue straight on along the SS242 for the Passo Sella. Follow this all the way to the Val di Fassa, then at the roundabout turn right into Canazei. From here follow the SS48 west in the direction of Moena to reach Campitello in 3km. Halfway through the village on the right there is a white and blue *rosticceria* (a butcher's shop that specialises in cooked meat). Turn right just past the building, following signs for the Val Duron. Almost immediately the road swings left over a bridge; don't follow this and instead continue straight ahead over the cobbles for 100 metres to reach a crossroad. Continue straight across and pass Hotel Cesa Riz to reach some roadside parking spaces near a large wooden plaque offering information on the Val Duron (the final section of road is quite steep and can be difficult to drive up with fresh snow). Allow around an hour for the drive between Monte Pana and Campitello.

From the parking area cross the bridge and ascend steeply up the large track (this is facilitated by a rope on the right which is useful in icy conditions), following signs for Rifugio Micheluzzi. After 1.5km reach **Rifugio Baita Fraines**. Immediately after this a small path branches off left signed for Val Duron. There are two options here: the smaller path leading off left through the woods runs parallel to the larger track. This path is arguably more interesting than the track, but it is more challenging route finding if the path isn't tracked.

Continue uphill along either the path or the large track for a further 30mins, still following signs for Rifugio Micheluzzi. Exit from the trees and enter into the valley proper, reaching **Rifugio Micheluzzi** which, sadly, is not open in the winter. From the rifugio, take path 532, which leads west along the valley floor with excellent views, passing a series of idyllic wooden huts and keeping on the right side of a frozen stream. Follow the valley for 80mins, ascending gently at first until the track becomes a path and begins to ascend more steeply until reaching the beautiful **Docoldaura farmhouse** on the right. Continue for another 20mins uphill

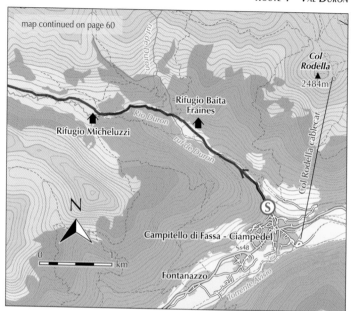

map continued on page 60

Col Rodella
2484m

Rifugio Baita Fraines

Rio Duron

rui de Duron

Rifugio Micheluzzi

Col Rodella cablecar

N

0   1 km

S

Campitello di Fassa - Ciampedel
ss48

Fontanazzo

Torrente Avisio

In the upper half approaching Passo Duron

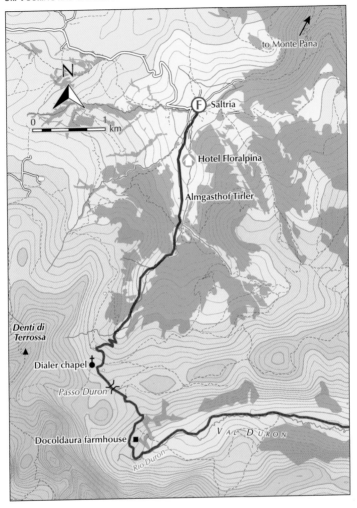

to reach the **Passo Duron** and spectacular views of the Alpe di Siusi and Odle/
Puez groups. Turn right here, descending for 10mins to the copse of trees hiding
the secluded **Dialer chapel**.

Denti di Terrossa

Passo Duron

Docoldaura farmhouse

Rifugio Micheluzzi

The descent continues along path 8, clearly signed to Saltria. This follows the right-hand side of the chapel perimeter fence for 100 metres before turning right at a junction, still following for Saltria along path 8. From here, descend a wide summer vehicle track which switchbacks down the hillside before following the valley floor past **Almgasthof Tirler** (a great spot for a well earned drink) and **Hotel Floralpina** to reach the tiny hamlet of **Saltria** in an hour.

From Saltria, if you have left your vehicle in Monte Pana, return on the ski bus, which runs frequently during the week, less so on Saturday and intermittently on a Sunday.

ROUTE 5
Forcella Sassolungo Nord

Start	Sasso Levante chairlift top (2170m)
Finish	Monte Pana (1610m)
Distance	6km
Total ascent	340m
Total descent	900m
Grade	F 2.2
Time	3–4hrs
Aspect of ascent	S
Aspect of descent	N
Map	Tabacco No 05
Equipment	Ski crampons/crampons
Return to start	A ski pass is required to return to the start with ease. From Monte Pana take the Monte Seura chairlift towards Sassolungo, descend the short blue run ahead then take the Tramans chairlift. Rejoin the Sella Ronda pistes and follow these anti-clockwise to return to the start of the route (1hr).
Parking	Passo Sella Dolomiti Mountain Resort hotel car park: 46.50901, 11.75765

This excellent itinerary skis the spectacular north facing valley that carves through the centre of the Sassolungo group, one of the most distinctive rock massifs in the area. The ascent takes place close to the Sella Ronda lift system but once at Forcella Sassolungo the landscape is transformed into a remote and fascinating environment, which often offers superb snow. The route requires a stable snowpack and it's important to keep an eye on the time if returning via the ski lifts of Monte Pana.

APPROACH

The route is generally approached using the pistes of the Sella Ronda to access the Sasso Levante chairlift directly under the south faces of Sassolungo. The

Sasso Levante lift enables a traverse into the route and saves some height gain. To access the lift by car, from Canazei take the SS48 leading north out of the village following signs for Passo Pordoi. After 6km reach a junction and turn left onto the SS242. Follow the road for a further 6km to reach the top of the Passo Sella. Continue down the other side for just under 1km to reach the Passo Sella Dolomiti Mountain Resort hotel and park in either of the car parks. The Sasso Levante chairlift departs from behind the hotel complex. To avoid using the lift, it is possible to skin up along the area just off the right side of the piste to reach the slope underneath Forcella Sassolungo (40mins).

From the top of the lift ski down into the wide area beneath Sassolungo, keeping as much height as possible. Put skins on and ascend the steep slope directly under the cables of the summer lift, aiming for the large and obvious saddle. Keep to the right side and ascend for an hour to reach **Forcella Sassolungo** and **Rifugio Demetz** (2681m). If the conditions are icy, crampons may be required towards the top.

Sasso Piatto
(2969m)

Cinque Dita
(2918m)

Forcella
Sassolungo

Sassolungo
(3181m)

Sasso Levante
chairlift top station

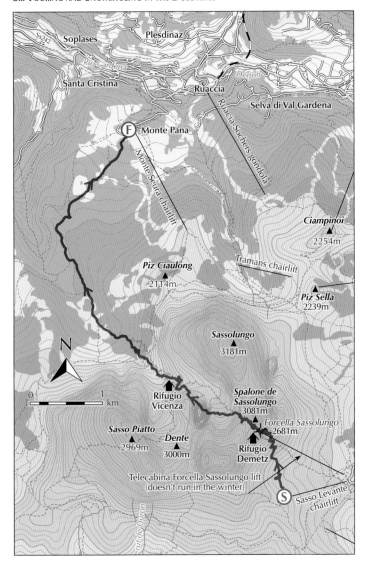

Deep powder in the lower half of the descent

Pass the rifugio to take in the first true glimpse of the valley. Take off the skins and ski northwards, descending carefully with many rocks forcing the way. Generally speaking the descent is easier towards the left side of the valley for the steeper initial section, but pick the best line depending on the conditions and snow cover. As the gradient eases the valley widens to allow a great ski with many possible lines, reaching a point just below **Rifugio Vicenza** on the left. Continue past the rifugio, now skiing northwest and following the valley down on its right-hand side to reach some sparse trees where the gradient eases. Keep angling rightwards to descend along the summer path 525; this is quite undulating and requires several sections of poling to eventually reach the road connecting Monte Pana and Saltria. Turn right and walk down the road for 10mins (with good snow cover this can be skated on skis) until the cross country pistes come into view on the left. Skate along these to return to the lift system at Monte Pana.

Other possibilities

For a longer day, it is worth considering Forcella del Dente (3.3) to the west which links several remote couloirs to join up with this classic itinerary at Rifugio Vicenza.

CANAZEI AND ARABBA: SELLA GROUP

Skiing down Canale del Ghiacciaio in perfect conditions (Route 7)

INTRODUCTION

The huge plateau of the Sella Massif is often referred to as the 'heart of the Dolomites' and lies squarely in the middle of the four Ladin valleys of Fodom, Fascia, Badia and Gherdëina. During the summer months the four passes (Pordoi, Sella, Gardena and Campolongo) encircling the group play host to thousands of road cyclists, while during the winter months the Sella Ronda – a 44km circular network of lifts and pistes that can be completed in either direction – draws many visitors from around the world. The circuit is well signed and can be completed in roughly 4–6 hours, depending on lift queues, chosen route and navigation. The piste network in the area is vast; it is well worth picking up a piste map if you're thinking of undertaking any of the routes in the area. These are readily available at ski pass offices, tourist offices and larger lift stations.

Perched above the busy pistes encompassing the massif lies a complex system of slopes, couloirs and open snow fields that are perfect for providing a range of exceptional ski tours that traverse some remote and impressive terrain. The most frequented and arguably famous of these is the Val Mesdì, a steep-sided valley that carves through the heart of the group and serves as an accessible yet spectacular itinerary that is achievable by many groups in the correct conditions. Just don't expect to get it to yourself!

The routes are all accessed via the Sass Pordoi cablecar, which lies equidistant between the two superbly situated towns of Canazei and Arabba. Located to the west at the head of the Val di Fassa lies Canazei, which is the larger of the two, offering slightly more in the way of amenities but at an increased cost. Arabba to the east by contrast has a more rustic feel and will appeal to those looking for a quieter experience. Both are well equipped for winter tourism however and provide good access to the other areas described – see in particular Canazei (Val di Fassa); Ortisei and Selva (Val Gardena); and Corvara (South Badia).

ROUTE 6
Val Mesdì

Start	Pordoi cablecar top station (2950m)
Finish	Corvara pistes (1600m)
Distance	8km
Total ascent	150m
Total descent	1500m
Grade	F 2.3
Time	2–3hrs
Aspect of ascent	N
Aspect of descent	N
Map	Tabacco No 07
Return to start	A ski pass is required to return to the start with ease. Follow the Sella Ronda in either direction to return to the car park at the bottom of the Pordoi cablecar (2hrs).
Parking	Pordoi cablecar car park: 46.48817, 11.81039

The Val Mesdì takes its name from the Ladin word for midday, so-called because it only gets the sun around noon. Carving its way through the heart of the Sella Massif, the valley is arguably the most famous touring route of the area and is often described as the Vallée Blanche of the Dolomites. The relative ease of access, north facing aspect often offering powder snow and dramatic landscape make for a stunning itinerary. Despite being very well travelled, the initial couloir should not be underestimated, nor should the approach in bad visibility. The popularity of the route means the narrower sections (in particular the upper couloir and the final section to the valley floor) are often quickly tracked out, although it is still often possible to get fresh tracks through the main valley which provides the meat of the route.

APPROACH

The ski tours on the Sella are accessed via the Pordoi cablecar, located equidistant between Arabba and Canazei atop the Passo Pordoi (SR48/SS48). The cablecar is most commonly accessed via the neighbouring lifts and as all of the descents lead back to the ski pistes of the Sella Ronda, the return home is usually straightforward. Take the cablecar, which runs roughly every 15mins to the top station.

In good visibility much of the tour can be viewed from the top of the cablecar station and the way is often well tracked to the northeast. Ski northeast and descend gently for 300 metres, following poles marking the summer path (note the funnel leading into Canale Holzer (5.1) on the left) until making a sharp turn to the right towards **Rifugio Forcella Pordoi**. The descent to the rifugio often gets stepped out, with large moguls and a small cornice to negotiate.

From **Forcella Pordoi** (which forms the start of two other popular ski tours not included in this guide, Forcella Pordoi (2.3) on the right which leads back to the bottom of the cablecar and Val Lasties (2.3) on the left) sidestep up on the other side of the rifugio, passing above a wooden shrine and rounding a corner to the right. Ski down to the east, keeping as much speed as possible until reaching a steeper uphill section. Put skins on here and kick turn up the slope in front, heading northeast towards the summit of Piz Boè. Just below the top of the slope traverse to the left, following winter stakes to reach a large flat area underneath **Piz Boè**. Follow the natural slope of the valley northwards. The approach to Canale

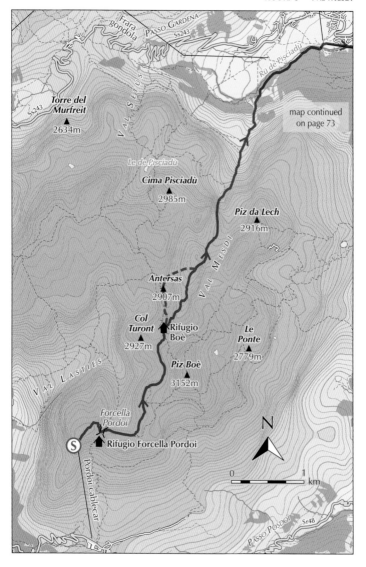

map continued on page 73

Torre del
Murfreit
▲
2634m

Le de Pisciadu

Cima Pisciadu
▲
2985m

Piz da Lech
▲
2916m

Antersas
▲
2907m

Col
Turont
▲
2927m
▲ Rifugio
Boè

Le
Ponte
▲
2779m

Piz Boè
▲
3152m

Forcella
Pordoi
Ⓢ ▲ Rifugio Forcella Pordoi

Pordoi cablecar

N

0   1
km

71

del Ghiacciaio (Route 7) turns right here up the southwest ridge of Piz Boè to reach the summit. Traverse and then descend a little to enter into a small valley underneath the west face of Piz Boè. Ascend the slope directly in front, still marked by winter stakes, to reach **Rifugio Boè** in 45mins from the cablecar station. Access towards the Antersas couloir descent starts from this point.

The couloir entering the Val Mesdì starts at the saddle just to the right (northeast) of the rifugio, providing a view down the length of this more difficult section. Ski down carefully until the valley opens out to allow the first proper view of this spectacular itinerary. There are now many possible lines although the best skiing is often found by repeatedly traversing up high along the slopes on the left or right side to drop back into the valley.

Towards the end of the valley the cliffs above Colfosco force the route along the streambed as it makes a slight turn to the right. Here the terrain is narrow, littered with small boulders and often well tracked, requiring a cautious descent.

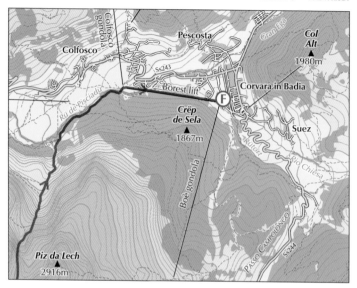

Just before reaching the gentle gradient of the valley floor below, stay on the right side of the stream to descend awkwardly down to a pisted track. Follow this to the right for 500 metres (watch out for walkers and cross county skiers) until a bridge leading left over the river. Cross this and continue to the **Borest lift** coming up from Corvara.

Antersas couloir from Rifugio Boè into the Val Mesdì

The Antersas couloir (4.1) provides an easily accessible alternative for experienced parties looking for a more challenging descent into the Val Mesdì. From **Rifugio Boè** head northwards following signposts for path 666 to make a short ascent to the rounded summit of **Antersas** (2907m). Ski down the opposite side to reach a flatter area where the couloir can be found on the right. The entrance is sometimes complicated by a large cornice and often requires the use of a rope. Ski down the first difficult section which is steep and narrow before the couloir widens to provide an excellent descent on often excellent snow down into the Val Mesdì.

Other possibilities

Route 7 provides a longer and more complete itinerary for those looking to access the summit of Piz Boè (3152m).

ROUTE 7

Canale del Ghiacciaio

Start	Pordoi cablecar top station (2950m)
Finish	Corvara pistes (1600m)
Distance	9km
Total ascent	400m
Total descent	1750
Grade	PD 3.2
Time	3–4hrs
Aspect of ascent	SW
Aspect of descent	N
Map	Tabacco No 07
Equipment	Crampons, ice axe
Return to start	A ski pass is required to return to the start with ease. Follow the Sella Ronda in either direction to return to the car park at the bottom of the Pordoi cablecar (2hrs).
Parking	Pordoi cablecar car park: 46.48817, 11.81039

This seldom frequented but excellent itinerary is a longer variant of the Val Mesdì (Route 6) and accesses the valley from the neighbouring summit of Piz Boè (3152m), the highest peak on the Sella. The route is best done in good visibility to fully enjoy the stunning views from the summit and also to assist with route finding which isn't always obvious. The ascent to the summit of Piz Boè requires mountaineering experience and the steep second half of the ascent requires an absolutely safe snowpack.

APPROACH

The ski tours on the Sella are accessed via the Pordoi cablecar, located equidistant between Arabba and Canazei atop the Passo Pordoi (SR48/SS48). The cablecar is most commonly accessed via the neighbouring lifts and, as all of the descents lead back to the ski pistes of the Sella Ronda, the return home is usually straightforward. Take the cablecar, which runs roughly every 15mins to the top station.

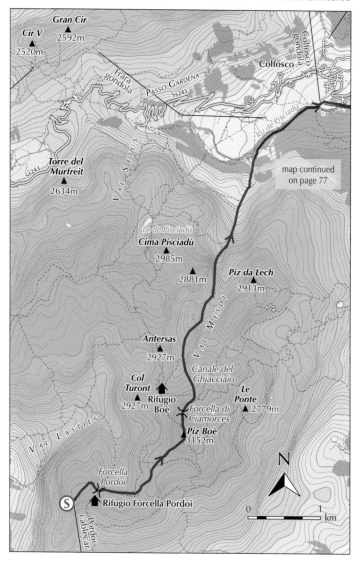

Cir V
2520m

Gran Cir
2592m

Frara gondola

PASSO GARDENA ss243

Colfosco gondola

Colfosco

Rü de Pisciadù

Torre del Murfreit
2634m

ss243

VAL SETUS

map continued on page 77

Le de Pisciadù

Cima Pisciadù
2985m

2881m

Piz da Lech
2913m

VAL MESDI

Antersas
2927m

Canale del Ghiacciaio

Col Turont
2927m

Rifugio Boè

Le Ponte
2779m

Forcella di Ciamorces

Piz Boè
3152m

VAL LASTIES

Forcella Pordoi

S Rifugio Forcella Pordoi

N

0   1 km

Pordoi cablecar

75

In good visibility much of the tour can be viewed from the top of the cablecar station and the way is often well tracked to the northeast. Ski northeast and descend gently for 300 metres, following poles marking the summer path (note the funnel leading into Canale Holzer (5.1) on the left) until making a sharp turn to the right towards **Rifugio Forcella Pordoi**. The descent to the rifugio often gets stepped out, with large moguls and a small cornice to negotiate.

From **Forcella Pordoi** (which forms the start of two other popular ski tours, Forcella Pordoi (2.3) on the right which leads back to the bottom of the cablecar and Val Lasties (2.3) on the left) sidestep up on the other side of the rifugio, passing above a wooden shrine and rounding a corner to the right. Ski down to the east, keeping as much speed as possible until reaching a steeper uphill section. Put skins on here and kick turn up the slope in front, heading northeast towards the summit of Piz Boè. Just below the top of the slope traverse to the left, following winter stakes to reach a large flat area underneath Piz Boè.

Proceed to the base of the southwest ridge and ascend this using crampons, following the summer path marked by short sections of cable and picking the best line with occasional short detours to the left and right to avoid the steeper sections before reaching the summit of **Piz Boè**. The elegant peak is marred slightly by the mobile phone relay but still provides wonderful views in all directions.

To descend, pass between Rifugio Capanna Fassa and the mobile phone relay and traverse just under the highest point of the ridge in front for 200 metres or so until reaching a saddle (**Forcella di Ciamorces**). From here, drop into the valley to the right (east), negotiating a cornice which can be quite large at times. Ski down the next steep slope to arrive just below the line of cliffs on the left-hand side. Here, traverse left directly under the cliffs for roughly 150 metres until a gap between the rock bands up on the left comes into view. Ascend this steep slope with care to reach a saddle overlooking a large open slope above **Canale del Ghiacciaio**.

Ski down the valley, often on beautiful snow, and pass a bottleneck between some small rock bands on the left before entering into the main couloir leading down into the Val Mesdì itself. There are now many possible lines although the best skiing is often found by repeatedly traversing up high along the slopes on the left or right side to drop back into the valley.

Towards the end of the valley the cliffs above Colfosco force the route along the streambed as it makes a slight turn to the right. Here the terrain is narrow, littered with small boulders and often well tracked, requiring a cautious descent. Just before reaching the gentle gradient of the valley floor below, stay on the right side of the stream to descend awkwardly down to a pisted track. Follow this to the right for 500 metres (watch out for walkers and cross county skiers) until a bridge leading left over the river. Cross this and continue to the **Borest lift** coming up from Corvara.

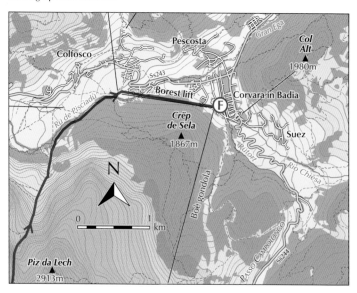

Approaching the summit of Piz Boè with views over the Marmolada (3343m)

ROUTE 8
Canale Col Anton into Val Lasties

Start	Pordoi cablecar top station (2950m)
Finish	Rifugio Pian Schiavaneis (1850m)
Distance	7km
Total ascent	100m
Total descent	1200m
Grade	F 3.3
Time	2–3hrs
Aspect of ascent	N
Aspect of descent	SW
Map	Tabacco No 07
Return to start	A ski pass is required to return to the start with ease. After walking to the Sella Ronda (see the end of the route description for details), follow it anti-clockwise (green) to return to the car park at the bottom of the Pordoi cablecar.
Parking	Pordoi cablecar car park: 46.48817, 11.81039

The Val Lasties is a beautiful valley, which splits the southwest side of the Sella Massif, serving as a popular freeride descent for skiers departing from the Pordoi cablecar. The inclusion of Canale Col Anton makes for a more complete itinerary, offering a short tour before entering the valley from further north via a striking and aesthetic west facing couloir.

APPROACH

The ski tours on the Sella are accessed via the Pordoi cablecar, located equidistant between Arabba and Canazei atop the Passo Pordoi (SR48/SS48). The cablecar is most commonly accessed via the neighbouring lifts and as all of the descents lead back to the ski pistes of the Sella Ronda, the return home is usually straightforward. Take the cablecar, which runs roughly every 15mins to the top station.

In good visibility much of the tour can be viewed from the top of the cablecar station and the way is often well tracked to the northeast. Ski northeast and descend gently for 300 metres, following poles marking the summer path (note the funnel

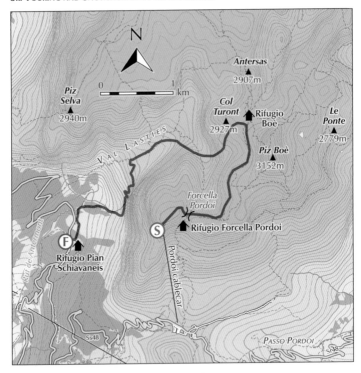

leading into Canale Holzer (5.1) on the left) until making a sharp turn to the right towards **Rifugio Forcella Pordoi**. The descent to the rifugio often gets stepped out, with large moguls and a small cornice to negotiate.

From **Forcella Pordoi** (which forms the start of two other popular ski tours not included in this guide, Forcella Pordoi (2.3) on the right which leads back to the bottom of the cablecar and Val Lasties (2.3) on the left) sidestep up on the other side of the rifugio, passing above a wooden shrine and rounding a corner to the right. Ski down to the east, keeping as much speed as possible until reaching a steeper uphill section. Put skins on here and kick turn up the slope in front, heading northeast towards the summit of Piz Boè. Just below the top of the slope traverse to the left, following winter stakes to reach a large flat area underneath **Piz Boè**. Follow the natural slope of the valley northwards. The approach to Canale del Ghiacciaio (Route 7) turns right here up the southwest ridge of Piz Boè to reach the summit. Traverse and then descend a little to enter into a small valley underneath the west face of Piz Boè. Ascend the slope in front to reach a shallow saddle overlooking **Rifugio Boè**. From here do an about turn and descend direct to reach the top of Canale Col Anton couloir (it is also possible to traverse in without making the final climb to the saddle but care must be taken not to drop too far down).

The couloir is wider than first appearances might suggest and unfolds at a steep but enjoyable gradient, passing several impressive icefalls on the left before opening out in the Val Lasties itself. From here traverse high on the right, skiing back down to the valley floor as it swings round to the left. Overcome a flatter area with a small uphill section at the end until it becomes possible to descend down the summer path 647 which strikes out leftwards towards the large black cliff of Sass Pordoi. Do not be tempted to follow the middle of the valley which contains a number of rocky cliffs that are difficult to spot from above. Negotiate a small boulderfield and keep left to either enter into a shallow gully down underneath the face or to reach a more open slope just to the right. Continue until uphill terrain forces a bend to the right then descend to a streambed. Follow the stream on its left-hand side to reach the road and **Rifugio Pian Schiavaneis** and Monte Pallidi, both offering excellent options for some refreshment.

To continue to the pistes, follow a path on the left-hand side of the road that leads into the woods, ascending and then descending to reach the Passo Pordoi

Perfect snow on the final section of trees in the Val Lasties

road. Cross this and continue down through the woods, staying on the left-hand side of the road to reach the ski pistes at Lupo Bianco. This cut-through takes 10–15mins.

Other possibilities
It is possible to ski the Val Lasties as a freeride itinerary without any ascent by dropping into the valley from **Forcella Pordoi** (2.3).

If Canale Col Anton isn't in good condition it is possible to continue to **Rifugio Boè** and ski either the Val Mesdì (Route 6) or Val Setus (Route 9).

ROUTE 9
Val Setus

Start	Pordoi cablecar top station (2950m)
Finish	Corvara pistes (2000m)
Distance	8km
Total ascent	350m
Total descent	1300m
Grade	F 3.3
Time	3–4hrs
Aspect of ascent	S/N
Aspect of descent	N
Map	Tabacco No 07
Return to start	A ski pass is required to return to the start with ease. Follow the Sella Ronda in either direction to return to the car park at the bottom of the Pordoi cablecar (2hrs).
Parking	Pordoi cablecar car park: 46.48817, 11.81039

Much like the neighbouring Val Mesdì (Route 6), the Val Setus is one of the classic descents of the Sella group and indeed the Dolomites. Although the tour across the vast plateau of the Sella is long, it doesn't present a huge amount of ascent and so provides a good opportunity to admire the spectacular setting. The initial couloir should not be underestimated but, having overcome this tricky section, a beautiful descent in often superb powder awaits.

APPROACH

The ski tours on the Sella are accessed via the Pordoi cablecar, located equidistant between Arabba and Canazei atop the Passo Pordoi (SR48/SS48). The cablecar is most commonly accessed via the neighbouring lifts and as all of the descents lead back to the ski pistes of the Sella Ronda, the return home is usually straightforward. Take the cablecar, which runs roughly every 15mins to the top station.

In good visibility much of the tour can be viewed from the top of the cablecar station and the way is often well tracked to the northeast. Ski northeast and descend gently for 300 metres, following poles marking the summer path (note the funnel leading into Canale Holzer (5.1) on the left) until making a sharp turn to the right towards **Rifugio Forcella Pordoi**. The descent to the rifugio often gets stepped out, with large moguls and a small cornice to negotiate.

From **Forcella Pordoi** (which forms the start of two other popular ski tours not included in this guide, Forcella Pordoi (2.3) on the right which leads back to the bottom of the cablecar and Val Lasties (2.3) on the left) sidestep up on the other side of the rifugio, passing above a wooden shrine and rounding a corner to the right. Ski down to the east, keeping as much speed as possible until reaching a steeper uphill section. Put skins on here and kick turn up the slope in front, heading northeast towards the summit of Piz Boè. Just below the top of the slope traverse to the

left, following winter stakes to reach a large flat area underneath **Piz Boè**. Follow the natural slope of the valley northwards. The approach to Canale del Ghiacciaio (Route 7) turns right here up the southwest ridge of Piz Boè to reach the summit.

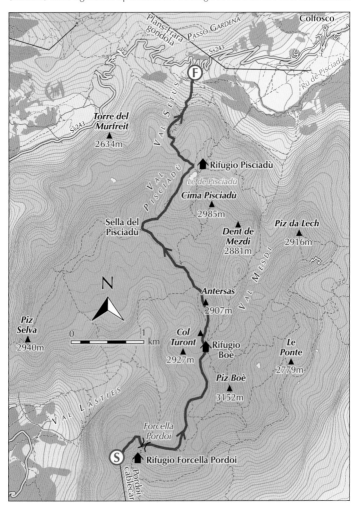

Sas da Lech
(2936m)

Descent from
couloir down
Val Setus

Traverse and then descend a little to enter into a small valley underneath the west face of Piz Boè. Ascend the slope directly in front, still marked by winter stakes, to reach **Rifugio Boè** in 45mins from the cablecar station.

Pass the rifugio and the entrance to the Val Mesdì (2.3) (Route 6) on the right and continue north, signed for path 666 and make a short ascent to reach the rounded summit of Antersas (2907m). Ski down the opposite side (better to keep skins on) to reach a flatter area. This is the entrance to Canale Antersas (4.1) which

Crossing the vast Sella plateau

leads into the Val Mesdì on the right. Continue in the same line until reaching a summer signpost; here turn left following the sign for path 649, which traverses underneath a small set of cliffs to arrive at **Sella del Pisciadù**.

The **Val Pisciadù** is now clearly visible to the right. Drop into the valley on the right side (there is often a cornice to negotiate here) and ski down towards **Rifugio Pisciadù**. If the snow conditions are safe, traverse up high on the left, aiming for an area of large boulders to the left of the rifugio. If the conditions aren't suitable for the traverse, ski down to Rifugio Pisciadù and then skin back up reach the boulders. Traverse to the west, staying high up on the left and ignoring the first evident couloir (the summer path 666 descends here). Pass underneath an overhead wire and make an exposed traverse above the next couloir to where it becomes possible to ski the fall line down into the couloir itself.

The couloir is less challenging than first appearances might suggest, although the initial steep section should not be underestimated and requires good snow conditions for a satisfying and safe descent. Once out of the initial couloir the valley opens out to provide a beautiful descent with often superb snow. On nearing the Passo Gardena the terrain narrows again; here follow the logical line between the rock walls to reach the ski piste just below the pass.

Other possibilities

If the cornice at the head of the Val Pisciadù is impassable it is possible to enter the valley using the Val de Tita, which descends to the west of Cima Pisciadù (3.2). This option requires good snow cover as well as a safe snowpack to traverse to the Pisciadù hut after the initial descent.

ORTISEI AND SELVA:
VAL GARDENA

Making the steep ascent with many kick turns up to Forcella di Mesdì (Route 13)

INTRODUCTION

Stretching east for 13 miles from the Passo Gardena on the northwestern corner of the Sella massif to the picturesque town of Ortisei, the Val Gardena is renowned for its skiing, climbing and woodcarving heritage. The Saslong slopes above Santa Cristina are home to the men's Super G in the FIS Ski World Cup, usually held in December, while the easy access to the Sella Ronda, Alpe di Siusi and the Furnes-Seceda ski areas makes the valley an attractive and convenient destination for piste skiers.

The Alpe di Siusi is the largest high alpine meadow in Europe and in summer is an idyllic green plateau dotted with wooden huts and interwoven with a labyrinth of accessible footpaths and tracks. From December to April the gentle slopes are transformed into a wintery paradise of piste skiing, snowshoeing and winter walking. Although the plateau has been heavily developed by the ski industry, the view over towards the Sassolungo group, the dramatic Denti di Terrarossa ridge and the two characteristic spires of Punta Euringer Punta Santer more than compensate from the manmade eyesore of Compaccio.

On the other side of the valley, the Geisler/Odle group is home to two superb mid-grade ski tours, Forcella della Roa and Forcella di Mesdì, both travelling through a dramatic and unspoilt landscape and providing an exhilarating descent for experienced skiers.

The main key bases in the Val Gardena are Selva in Val Gardena, Santa Cristina and Ortisei. Although Selva arguably benefits from the best location in terms of piste skiing and road access to other areas, Santa Cristina and Ortisei are perhaps more picturesque. The idyllic Vallunga lies above Selva, a steep-sided valley featuring an excellent cross country ski piste and home to a number of challenging ice and mixed climbs. The valley is also a superb destination for a gentle winter stroll and forms the exits from the Val de Chedul (Route 15) and Forcella de Ciampei (Route 16) ski tours (included in the Corvara – South Badia section of this guide).

The three villages offer excellent amenities, accommodation and restaurant options and are well connected to the other Dolomite valleys by car or via the popular Sella Ronda ski circuit. Thanks to the railway station at Ponte Gardena, just 14km west of Ortisei, the area can also be accessed easily by rail with direct trains from Verona, Bolzano and Bressanone.

ROUTE 10
Compaccio

Start/Finish	Siusi allo Sciliar lift top station (1844m)
Distance	14km
Total ascent	250m
Total descent	250m
Grade	E
Time	4–5hrs
Aspect of ascent	N
Aspect of descent	N
Map	Tabacco No 05
Parking	Siusi allo Sciliar lift station car park: 46.54009, 11.56532

A pretty ramble which, despite beginning from the somewhat overdeveloped resort of Compaccio, soon leaves the lifts behind and travels through a scenic winter wonderland of idyllic mountain farms and snowy pastures.

APPROACH

From Selva, follow the SS242 west towards Bolzano, passing through the villages of Santa Cristina and Ortisei. Shortly after leaving Ortisei, turn left onto Strada Digon/SS64 signed towards Bulla/Pufels, Castelrotto and the Alpe di Siusi, passing through a tunnel. Follow this for 11.5km, passing through the village of Castelrotto to reach a junction, where Bolzano is signed to the right. Keep left here, now following the SP24 for 2km to enter into the village of Siusi allo Sciliar. Once in the village, follow signs for the Alpe di Siusi (marked by a cablecar symbol) which lead out of the village and to a junction leading left to the large car parks of the gondola station. Take the gondola to reach Compaccio.

Turn right out of the gondola to a crossroads, then continue straight on onto the well-pisted track which ascends steadily in the direction of the dramatic ridge-line of the Denti di Terrarossa, crossing under the **Panorama chairlift** and passing

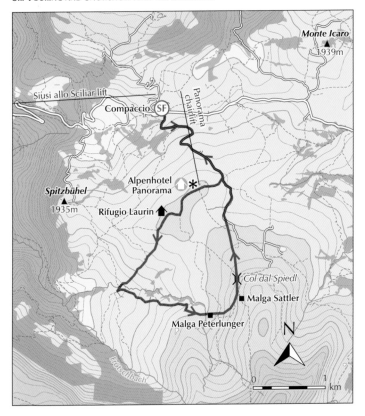

Rifugio Santner on the left before bearing right to reach **Alpenhotel Panorama** and the top of the chairlift.

From the hotel follow summer signs for path 6, passing alongside **Rifugio Laurin** and continuing across the snowy plateau to reach a signpost marking the junction with path 5 by the stream. Turn left here leaving the waymarks behind and taking a line just to the right side of the stream on often untracked snow to reach the idyllic farm buildings of **Malga Peterlunger**. Here the waymarks return, now following path 13 towards the next farm, **Malga Sattler**. A short ascent from here leads to **Col dal Spiedl**, entering back into the ski lift network by the Punta d'Oro lift.

Negotiating deep snow in the middle of the route

Follow path 2 which keeps to the left of the lifts and leads back down to Alpenhotel Panorama. From here retrace your steps down the pisted track to return to the gondola station.

ROUTE 11
Alpe di Siusi traverse

Start	Williams Hütte (2100m)
Finish	Saltria (1700m)
Distance	10km
Total ascent	200m
Total descent	600m
Grade	F
Time	4–5hrs
Aspect of ascent	N
Aspect of descent	N
Map	Tabacco No 05
Parking	Monte Pana car park: 46.55145, 11.71611

This is a superb and remote route, which traverses above the vast alpine plateau of the Alpe di Siusi (Seiser Alm), offering excellent views into the Catinaccio, Odle and Puez groups before arriving at the beautifully secluded Dialer chapel. Given that the route is predominantly a traverse, a safe snowpack and good navigational skills are essential, especially if the path isn't tracked.

APPROACH

Saltria is best accessed via bus from Monte Pana. (See map in Route 5 for location of Monte Pana.) From Ortisei to the west or Selva to the east, reach the village of Santa Cristina along the SS242. From Santa Cristina, Monte Pana is well signposted along a very steep and narrow road; in snowy conditions it can be worth considering leaving the car at the bottom of the hill and taking the chairlift that leads up to Monte Pana. If braving the road, park in any of the several large car parks at the top. The bus stop to Saltria is located on the road between the chairlift on the left and the nursery slopes on the right. The buses run frequently during the week, less so on Saturday and intermittently on a Sunday. The bus journey takes 15mins and leads to the Florian chairlift; take this to reach Williams Hütte.

To avoid taking the chairlift, it is possible to follow a staked path (number 7a) which skirts the left-hand side of the piste underneath the Florian chairlift, but this is not especially peaceful. From **Williams Hütte** at the top of the Florian chairlift

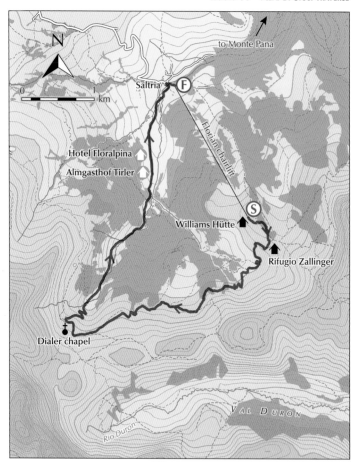

follow the piste downhill to the southeast, passing around the left side of a small hill until Rifugio Zallinger comes into view on the right, characterised by a small church. Walk down to **Rifugio Zallinger** (a beautiful if admittedly quite early spot for a drink) and pass the building on its right side, following the piste downhill for a further 50 metres before a sledging track (path number 9) leads off to the left.

Entering one of the many clearings as you start the long and beautiful traverse

Follow this downhill for 250 metres to reach another junction. Watch out for high speed tobogganists! Turn left here onto path 7, signed for Rifugio Alpe di Tires.

After a couple of minutes reach a farmhouse where the signs for path 7 indicate an abrupt left turn; in the absence of tracks navigation becomes rather difficult. Walk uphill for 20 metres in the direction of the signpost then turn right above a fence, aiming for a characteristic tree in the centre of the field with a red and white marker painted on the trunk. Continue past the tree in the same line, heading ever so slightly uphill to reach a small ravine after 5mins (if in doubt stay high). Follow the ravine downhill on its right side to reach a pair of small wooden bridges and cross these to reach the left-hand side. Follow the path for 5mins, initially ascending steeply and then traversing the hillside through dense woodland to reach a large open area.

Traverse across the open area, heading slightly uphill and passing underneath the wire of a goods cableway which serves a hut up on the left, ultimately aiming for a wooden bench just before an area of dense trees. The bench is sometimes buried after heavy snowfall and can be hard to spot. Just above the bench the path re-enters the woodland and begins to traverse until reaching yet another large open area with some beautiful wooden huts down to the right. The summer path traverses the steep slope in front but in the winter it is often easier to drop down into the snowfield below before ascending just below the bank, aiming for a signpost in the top left corner of the field.

From here follow signs for Rifugio Molignon, rounding a small corner and then descending ever so slightly, aiming for a gap in the trees which leads into the next large open snowfield. Traverse this, staying above two large trees in the middle of the open area until arriving level with two huts at the bottom of the field and another signpost confirming the correct route on path 7.

The **panorama** is spectacular here, with far-reaching views taking in the vast plateau of the Alpe di Siusi unfolding below as well as Monte Castello, Punta Santner, the Odle and Puez groups and the distant peaks of the Austrian Alps.

Continue along the path as it gently ascends for 10mins before encountering another small ravine, which splits a broad plateau. There is a summer bridge leading across this although getting down to it can be difficult as the banks are steep and hard work in icy conditions. Cross the bridge and ascend onto the plateau, skirting above another small hollow. From here the navigation becomes easier as the small copse of trees that surrounds Dialer chapel is clearly visible to the west. Contour over the plateau, passing above a large farm building and reaching **Dialer chapel** in a further 10mins, constantly surrounded by excellent views to the south of the Molignon ridgeline and the start of the Catinaccio group.

ALPE DI SIUSI

At 56sq km, the Alpe di Siusi is the largest mountain plateau in Europe. Traditionally a remote farming community, the construction of the Brennero railway in 1867 brought an increasing number of wealthy visitors to the area. The owners of the alpine farms, known as 'Malga' and 'Alm' in Italian and German respectively, began to adapt their livelihoods to cater for this first wave of tourism, offering food, drink and sometimes basic accommodation. In 1935 a cablecar was constructed to connect the plateau to the town of Ortisei, followed by the first lifts in 1938. This development halted during the Second World War but recommenced soon after, developing in line with the boom in ski tourism and becoming the winter paradise it is today.

To begin the descent, follow signs for Saltria along path 8, skirting the right-hand side of the chapel perimeter fence for 100 metres until turning right at a junction, still following path 8 for Saltria. The descent takes a wide summer vehicle track that switchbacks down the hillside before following the valley floor past **Almgasthof Tirler** (another great place for a drink) and **Hotel Floralpina** to reach **Saltria** and the bus stop in 1hr.

ROUTE 12

Chiesetta di San Giacomo and Monte Pic

Start/Finish	Sacun (1440m)
Distance	9km
Total ascent	700m
Total descent	700m
Grade	F
Time	5–6hrs
Aspect of ascent	S
Aspect of descent	S
Map	Tabacco No 05
Equipment	The ascent occasionally requires crampons
Parking	Hotel Ansitz Jakoberhof: 46.57071, 11.6911

This long and demanding snowshoe takes in the beautiful church of Chiesetta di San Giacomo, perched above the Val Gardena, before ascending to the panoramic Monte Pic (2363m) and descending down past Malghe di Seurasas. The walk combines spectacular views over Sassolungo, Ortisei and the Val Gardena with picturesque and remote woodland. The ascent is steep, needs to be tackled with an absolutely safe snowpack and offers difficult route finding if the way has not already been tracked. The lower section is often free of snow for much of the season due to its relatively low altitude and south facing aspect. If in doubt, it is possible to complete the route in reverse as an out-and-back itinerary using path 20(a), which is safer and easier to navigate.

APPROACH

From Selva, drive along the Val Gardena to reach Ortisei. Stay on the main road and pass through the town, crossing through a short tunnel to reach a roundabout. Turn right here following signs for San Giacomo to reach a second roundabout in 100 metres. Turn right again, still following signs for San Giacomo and driving over cobbles towards the village centre. In 50 metres the village becomes a pedestrian only zone and the road swings to the left.

Continue along this, passing in front of the church and following the road for 1.5km as it begins to ascend steeply to reach Hotel Ansitz Jakoberhof on the left in the tiny hamlet of Sacun. There is very little space for parking – it is worth asking the hotel for permission to use their car park.

Take path 6b, clearly signposted on the right-hand side of the hotel, and follow it uphill for 15mins to reach the church of **Chiesetta di San Giacomo** – in the absence of tracks this requires some careful navigation, using the glimpses of the church spire through the trees as a reference.

The **church** itself is beautiful and it is well worth taking some time to explore the interior and surrounding grounds. The view looking southeast towards Sassolungo is particularly impressive and makes for a great landscape photo opportunity.

Take path 6, which leads up behind the church and is signposted towards Rifugio Seurasas and Monte Pic. Follow the path which ascends steeply uphill for 25mins, taking care to follow the sporadic path markers on the trees until arriving at **Balest** (1823m) and the junction with path 8 joining from the left. Here there are excellent views of Ortisei and the surrounding area – on a clear day the view

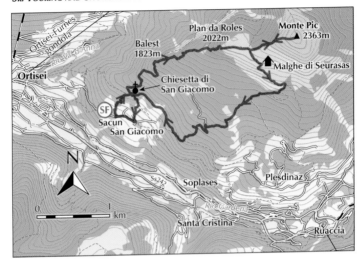

extends right across to the Austrian Alps. Turn right, staying on path 6 and still following signs for Monte Pic. Ascend a shoulder, just to the right of the cliff edge, for 15mins until reaching an open area. Cross this to reach **Plan da Roles** (2022m) and another junction with path 6a.

The idyllic church of San Giacomo

Turn right, staying on path 6 to view a long cliff face. Ascend the left side of this to reach a bench and a large cross. The vista is now outstanding, with far-reaching views over the Val Gardena and across to the Sella Group, Sassolungo, the Alpe di Siusi and Austria. Looking to the northeast the summit of Monte Pic is now clearly visible. Continue following the well signposted path 6 (ignoring path 20 which turns off right) up the left-hand ridge of **Monte Pic** (2363m) to reach the superbly panoramic summit in 45mins.

To descend, return to the base of the ridge and turn left onto path 20, following signs for Rifugio Seurasas, reached in a further 10mins. The hut is closed during the winter but the decking provides a lovely scenic spot for a rest and lunch. To continue, follow the staked track southeast, staying to the left and above a series of quaint huts and outbuildings.

Where the track turns southwest, keep right and join path 20a, following signs for San Giacomo. This joins up with path 4; follow this right to quickly arrive at another junction. Continue along path 4 to the hamlet of Pedracia and the road back to the car. Alternatively to visit San Giacomo again turn right onto path 32 to return to the church in 10mins.

ROUTE 13
Forcella di Mesdì

Start	Col Raiser gondola top station (2100m)
Finish	Seceda cablecar (1785m)
Distance	10km
Total ascent	700m
Total descent	1015m
Grade	F 3.1
Time	4–5hrs
Aspect of ascent	S
Aspect of descent	N
Map	Tabacco No 05
Equipment	Crampons
Return to start	From the Seceda cablecar it is possible to descend the piste to Ortisei or to take the cablecar up before skiing back down to the car park at the bottom of the Col Raiser gondola.
Parking	Col Raiser gondola car park: 46.56495, 11.73655

A spectacular and classic itinerary that breaches the stunning Odle (Geisler) peaks via a dramatic south facing couloir before descending the remote north side right on the edge of the Dolomites. The scenery is stunning throughout while the long and open descent often offers great powder snow. It is important to pick the right moment to ascend the steep south facing side to ensure a safe snowpack.

APPROACH

The usual approach is via the Col Raiser gondola out of Santa Cristina, which lies equidistant between Ortisei to the west and Selva to the east on the SS242. The lift station is well signposted and is served by a large attended car park (€5 for the day). For people staying in Ortisei the itinerary can be accessed using the Seceda cablecar out of the centre of town (see Other possibilities).

From the top of the Col Raiser gondola, the couloir is hidden but the line of ascent between Sass de Mesdì and the adjacent Sass Rigais to the right is easily identifiable. Put skins on straight away and follow the piste which descends to the northeast for 30 metres or so before branching off left to follow signposting for

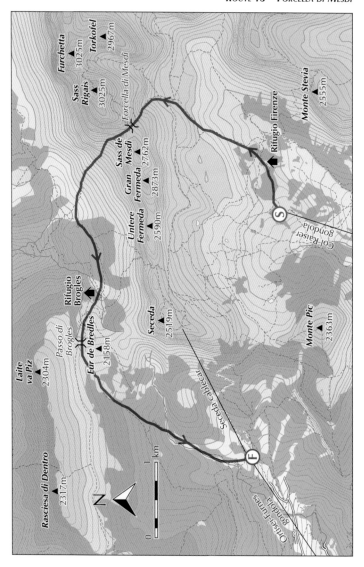

Rifugio Firenze along the summer path 4. The path follows a logical line and is nearly always tracked, leading to **Rifugio Firenze** in just under 15mins. Just before reaching the outhouses turn left at a prominent signpost and follow for Forcella di Mesdì on path 13 which leads uphill towards the Odle group. Follow winter stakes underneath a small band of cliffs and round to the right, ignoring a left turn for path 13b arriving at a large open area directly beneath the gap between Sass de Mesdì and Sass Rigais in around 40mins. At a signpost indicating Forcella di Mesdì, follow for path 29, which enters into the valley between the two peaks, first at a gentle gradient and then getting increasingly steeper and narrower. On nearing the saddle it may be necessary to bootpack the last few metres with crampons if conditions are icy.

From the saddle of **Forcella di Mesdì** the line of the descent can be easily observed. Descend the wide couloir, which soon leads to open slopes. Ski in the same line until reaching the forest below, aiming to join path 35 (Adolf Munkel Weg), which crosses the forest horizontally from west to east (this is a popular snowshoe itinerary and is usually well tracked). Keep descending to take the more direct route to Val di Funes. Put the skins back on and follow the track west for 35mins to reach the fantastically situated **Rifugio Brogles**, which unfortunately doesn't open in the winter. Continue past the rifugio for a further 10mins to reach **Passo di Brogles** and the end of the second part of ascent. From here, ski down path 5 which follows the bottom of a small valley, crossing the stream first to the

Sass Rigais
(3025m)

Sass de Mesdi
(2762m)

Descending the beautiful north facing slope down from Forcella di Mesdi

right and then the left following signs for the **Seceda cablecar**, reached in 15mins after a final short section of uphill along a pisted forestry track.

Other possibilities

The route can also be started from Ortisei, taking the **Ortisei-Furnes gondola** out of the town centre and then taking the **Seceda cablecar**. From here it is possible to traverse to the itinerary along summer paths 1 and 2b.

For a quicker descent, rather than traversing out along the Adolf Munkel Weg continue all the way down into the Val di Funes. This does complicate the return journey, however, as the Val di Funes is a long drive from either Santa Cristina or Ortisei and the journey on public transport is not straightforward.

Enjoying the south facing aspect in good snow (Route 25)

ROUTE 14
Forcella della Roa

Start	Col Raiser gondola top station (2100m)
Finish	Longiarù outskirts (1500m)
Distance	12km
Total ascent	600m
Total descent	1200m
Grade	E 3.1
Time	3–4hrs
Aspect of ascent	N
Aspect of descent	E
Map	Tabacco No 05
Return to start	Given the difficult logistics of a return using public transport, a car drop is recommended for this route.
Parking	Col Raiser gondola car park: 46.56495, 11.73655

A long and beautiful traverse through the Puez group, this route provides some of the best scenery in the area and will appeal to those who enjoy the journey just as much as the descent. The finish point is a long way from the start and the logistics of returning will need to be considered.

APPROACH

The usual approach is via the Col Raiser gondola out of Santa Cristina, which lies equidistant between Ortisei to the west and Selva to the east on the SS242. The lift station is well signposted and is served by a large attended car park (€5 for the day).

At the top of the Col Raiser gondola the view of the jagged Odle peaks to the northeast is immediately striking. Put skins on straight away and follow the piste which descends to the northeast for 30 metres or so before branching off left to follow signposting for Rifugio Firenze along the summer path 4. The path follows a logical line and is nearly always tracked, leading to the **Rifugio Firenze** in just under 15mins.

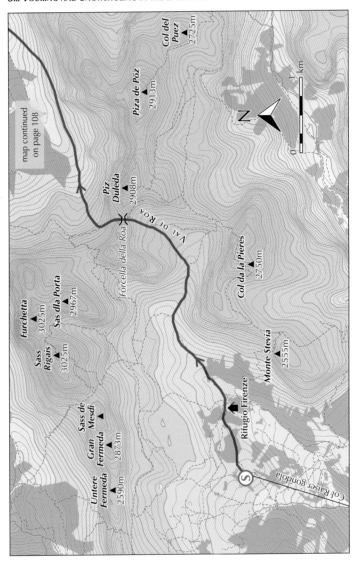

map continued on page 108

Follow signs for summer paths 2 and 3, which lead northeast from the rifugio up into the valley. Stay on the left side of the valley, avoiding the thicker vegetation to the right and eventually crossing the streambed, following the valley as

Traversing underneath the beautiful Odle group

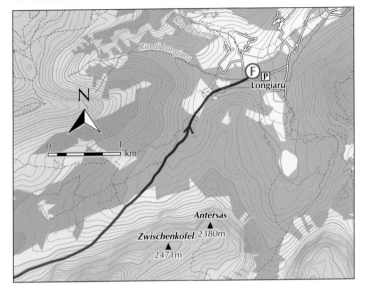

it bends round to the right (east). Follow this briefly until Val de Roa comes into view. Branch left into this and ascend the centre of the valley at a steeper but manageable gradient, angling to the right when the terrain allows. It is also possible to continue up the valley and take the next valley on the left. Towards the top of the valley Forcella della Roa becomes evident up to the right, accessed via a final steep slope.

The saddle of **Forcella della Roa** provides a good view of the descent to follow. The initial section is fairly steep and narrow before getting progressively wider and gentler as the descent continues. In good snow conditions it is possible to ski right from the top, otherwise it may be necessary to descend a little to drop below the scattered rocks. Descend northwards at first before turning northeast and entering into the main valley, following this on its right side and eventually joining the pisted track leading down to the parking area above **Longiarù**.

Other possibilities
In good snow conditions this route is equally interesting done in reverse.

CORVARA:
SOUTH BADIA

The initial descent from Forcella de Ciampei into Vallunga (Route 16)

INTRODUCTION

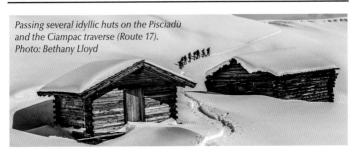

Passing several idyllic huts on the Pisciadù and the Ciampac traverse (Route 17).
Photo: Bethany Lloyd

Corvara is perhaps one of the best known resorts in the Dolomites. Its name derives from the Latin 'Corvus' added to the suffix '-aria', collectively meaning 'Place of the Ravens'. Famous for its privileged location on the Sella Ronda, the 44km piste circuit around the Sella Massif, it is dominated by the distinctive cylindrical summit of Sassongher. Although there are only five routes included in this section, the village is an ideal base for accessing almost all of the itineraries covered in this guidebook, with excellent road access to the Campolongo, Valparola and Passo Gardenaes and an extensive linked ski network.

The two ski tours included in this book are both easily accessed from the village, taking advantage of the lifts to gain some initial height before dropping dramatically into the open valley of Vallunga. The Val de Chedul in particular is an excellent route for beginners, involving a short but steep tour through stunning rock

spires before an enjoyable descent down the valley. The nearby Forcella de Ciampei requires more experience and consequently solitude is almost always guaranteed.

Served by two gondolas, the first accessing the open plateau of Pralongia and the second leading to Vallon below the upper walls of the Sella massif, Corvara is an excellent base for skiers as well, providing easy access to superb scenery and some truly excellent mountain huts. Corvara also boasts a cross country circuit, an ice rink and an outdoor artificial climbing wall.

The other villages of the Alta Badia are also very well developed for tourism and skiing in particular, with Colfosco, La Villa and San Cassiano also making excellent starting points. Badia is another option, a smaller village located to the north offering some accommodation options and providing some of the best access to the San Martino (North Badia and Fanis) area.

ROUTE 15
Val de Chedul and Col Toronn

Start	Rifugio Jimmy (2220m)
Finish	Vallunga (1620m)
Distance	7km
Total ascent	300m
Total descent	900m
Grade	F 2.2
Time	3–4hrs
Aspect of ascent	S
Aspect of descent	W
Map	Tabacco No 07
Return to start	A ski pass is required to return to the start with ease. Take the Val chairlift adjacent to Rifugio Ciampac at the entrance to Vallunga to rejoin the Sella Ronda pistes above Selva di Val Gardena. Follow the pistes back to Rifugio Jimmy or Colfosco as required.
Parking	Hotel Luianta car park: 46.55089, 11.84562

The Val de Chedul is a popular and beautiful valley that runs parallel to the larger Vallunga and offers an excellent easy ski descent in a fascinating environment. The valley can be accessed in numerous ways, although the one described here is arguably the most frequented. A detour up to the nearby peak of Col Toronn (2655m) is highly recommended both to extend the ski down and for the stunning views from the summit. The final section of the descent through the woods into Vallunga should not be underestimated, particularly if there is scant snow cover or if the route has not been well tracked.

The ice falls above the village of **Colfosco** are a popular destination for winter climbers, and can be viewed in all their splendour from the Cascate de Pisciadù Into Pra De Tru Forcelles snowshoe – just be careful not to get too close when there are climbers on the ice!

APPROACH

From Corvara take the SS243 signposted towards the Passo Gardena to reach the town of Colfosco in 2km, then take the Plans-Frara gondola up to Rifugio Jimmy (Jimmy Hütte) where the route begins.

From **Rifugio Jimmy** put skins on and ascend the slope to the northeast (right of the rifugio when looking at it head on), following signs for path 2 and keeping to the left of an area of dwarf pines. Reach a flatter area covered in rock towers and traverse through these, still heading north, aiming for Forcella Cir. This is reached after a short steep section which normally has to be tackled on foot and may be difficult to navigate in poor visibility as much of the landscape looks the same.

Col Toronn (2655m)

Rifugio Jimmy

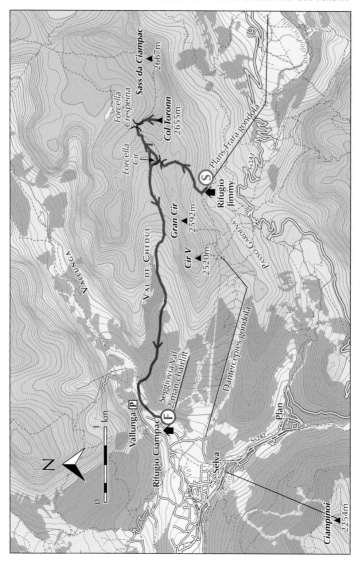

113

From the saddle of **Forcella Cir** the majority of the descent down Val de Chedul can be immediately observed. To descend without the detour to Col Toronn, ski northwest from here to drop into the valley bottom and start the descent. From the saddle head northeast, aiming for the valley floor directly below the ascending slope to the right. Put skins back on and climb up to just before **Forcella Crespeina** (easily identified by a large cross). From here a ridge leads up to the right (south) to reach the summit of **Col Toronn** and some fantastic views over the Sella and Val Gardena.

To descend, ski down your uphill tracks back to Forcella Crespeina, and into the **Val de Chedul**, following the valley floor and keeping to the left of a scattered boulderfield to avoid a small rocky drop halfway down the valley (many possible lines). Continue into sparse vegetation which becomes thicker towards the

Deep snow in the steep trees at the base of the Val de Chedul

bottom, following the cleared area of summer path 12 which enters the woods to the left. This final section through the trees is narrow, steep and requires good snow cover for an enjoyable descent. After you have negotiated this section the path leads out on the left-hand side of a stream into the broad Vallunga. Turn left and follow the cross country piste back to the **Seggiovia Val chairlift** at the bottom of the valley to link back to the main Sella Ronda lift system.

Other possibilities

If the visibility is poor or to start and finish in the same place, it is possible to ascend the valley from the parking area in Vallunga and then ski down your uphill tracks.

For a longer traverse it is possible to ascend from the Stella Alpina above Colfosco to Forcella de Ciampei (Route 16), then turn left to follow path 2 and traverse underneath **Sass da Ciampac** to reach **Forcella Crespeina** in a little over an hour. This enables a ski descent of the entire length of the **Val de Chedul** (2.2).

ROUTE 16
Forcella de Ciampei

Start	Stella Alpina lift top station (1920m)
Finish	Vallunga (1620m)
Distance	8km
Total ascent	450m
Total descent	750m
Grade	F 3.1
Time	3–4hrs
Aspect of ascent	S
Aspect of descent	NW
Map	Tabacco No 07
Return to start	A ski pass is required to return to the start with ease. Take the Seggovia Val chairlift adjacent to Rifugio Ciampac at the entrance to Vallunga to rejoin the pistes above Selva di Val Gardena. Follow the pistes back to Colfosco.
Parking	Skipass Colfosco car park: 46.55053, 11.85608

Despite using the Alta Badia and Val Gardena lift systems to start and finish this route, this beautiful traverse through the Puez group is rarely frequented and highly recommended. After the initial steep descent from Forcella de Ciampei the itinerary then joins up with the cross country track running through Vallunga, requiring good fitness, before leading back to the lift system.

APPROACH

This route is accessed using the Colfosco gondola and then the Stella Alpina button lift. From Corvara take the SS243 signposted towards the Passo Gardena to reach the town of Colfosco in 2km (parking on the left on entering the town). The gondola departs from just below the town.

From the top of the button, follow the summer path 4, ascending northwest up the centre of the valley with various waymarks and wooden path boundaries visible

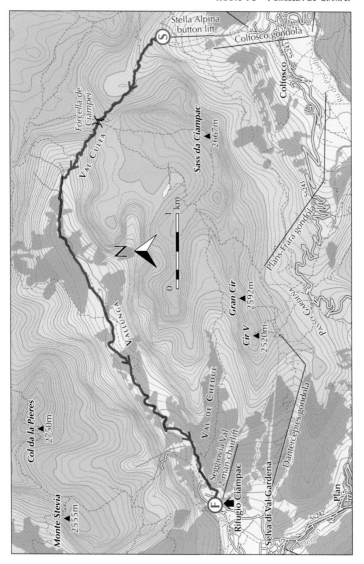

in sparse snow. After 20mins a small modern religious shrine marks a junction where the summer path to Sassongher bears right. Avoid this, keeping left and ascending more steeply until the terrain flattens into a bowl.

The col of Forcella de Ciampei is now clearly visible straight ahead to the northwest. If the snowpack is completely stable it is possible to traverse up high on the left, or if in doubt drop down into the bowl before ascending up the bottom of the valley with numerous kick-turns to reach **Forcella de Ciampei** in 45mins.

The descent begins immediately on the opposite side of the col, from where it is possible to look down the entire line of the **Val Culea** to check conditions. The first part is steeper and often offers hard snow, however the gradient eases further down and the snow usually improves, often offering superb powder snow with a continuous and uncomplicated descent all the way into the bottom of the wide and beautiful Vallunga. On reaching the flat area of the valley floor stay to the right of a small streambed, following the summer path (some poling may be required on many of the flatter sections) all the way down to the cross country tracks. Follow these downhill (many possible variations) to reach the **Seggovia Val chairlift** at the bottom of the valley.

Negotiating the final cornice to reach Forcella de Ciampei

Other possibilities

Forcella de Ciampei can be travelled as part of a long traverse to descend the Val Chedul (see Route 15), cutting right through the heart of the Puez group. Follow the approach as far as Forcella de Ciampei then turn left to follow path 2 and traverse underneath **Sass da Ciampac** to reach **Forcella Crespeina** in a little over an hour. From here it is possible to ski the entire length of the **Val Chedul** (2.2).

ROUTE 17

Pisciadù and the Ciampac traverse

Start/Finish	Corvara (1500m)
Distance	12km
Total ascent	350m
Total descent	700m
Grade	E
Time	4–5hrs
Aspect of ascent	N
Aspect of descent	S
Map	Tabacco No 07
Parking	Boè gondola car park: 46.54903, 11.87109

A stunning circular itinerary, this snowshoe combines two walks to take in exceptional views, a combination of terrain (from pisted tracks to deep untouched snow), an idyllic mountain rifugio and the beautiful church of Colfosco. The first section of the walk is well frequented and follows a pisted track while the second half is more remote and requires good navigational skills if the way isn't tracked.

APPROACH

Park in the centre of Corvara at the large pay and display car park below the Boè gondola.

From the car park, walk towards the ice rink then opposite this, just below the children's ski school, there is a collection of signposts pointing towards Cascate de Pisciadù, Tru dla Cascades and Colfosco. Follow these to cross below the ski school and the button lift, then in 50 metres reach the road just before Bar al Lago. Turn left, following the same signs to walk alongside the right side of the button lift.

Continue past a number of houses and hotels on the right. Where the path ends, follow the track sharply left then back right to another sign, leading below the gondola lift until reaching Colfosco campsite in 15mins. Skirt the campsite on the right and then where the path splits, keep left up into the woods, following signs for Cascate de Pisciadù and Tru dla Cascades. Ignore path 645 leading left and right and continue straight on along path 28, following the left side of the stream until reaching a junction with path 650 signposted off to the right in a clearing. Turn right onto this and continue over a snowy meadow, passing between the huts and eventually crossing the piste (watch out for skiers) to reach the bottom of the **Plans-Frara gondola**. Take this all the way (two stages – don't exit at the mid station!) to the top station at **Rifugio Jimmy** (Jimmy Hütte). Located in a stunning spot overlooking the Sella, this is an ideal spot for a coffee or some local cuisine.

Head back towards the lift and then walk to the right of the lift station for 20 metres to pick up a sign for path 8a, signed for the Edelweisstal, Colfosco and Corvara. Follow this, keeping just to the right of the gondola and resisting the temptation to stray too far right. Route finding can be a little complicated in heavy snow as many of the paint markers are on the ground, but as a reference, aim for the cluster of three gondola pylons where the gondola crests the lip of the hill and follow a path leading into a shallow valley just to the right of these.

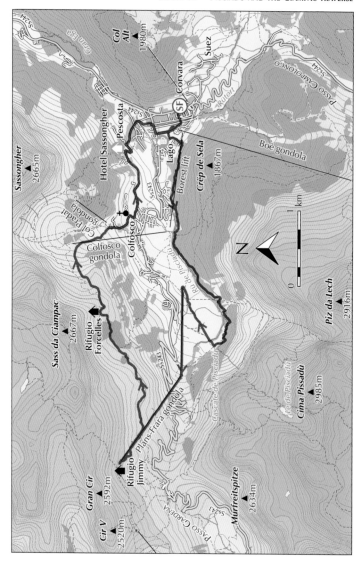

Follow the shallow valley with some steep sections until the gradient becomes gentler and it is possible to cut left underneath the gondola and cross between a rickety wooden hut on the left and a newer hut on the right, aiming for the national park sign 50 metres above the lower hut. The next section can be difficult to navigate without tracks: from the national park sign, continue uphill slightly along a crest, aiming for a prominent boulder with a painted waymark and a smaller boulder on the left. Skirt the left side of the rightmost boulder then follow the blunt ridge to the right, first on its left side and then on the right, picking the most logical line through the vegetation and snow to exit from the trees into an open area.

Continue traversing along path 8, following the natural topography of the hillside for 20mins and passing numerous wooden huts as the path weaves in and out of the trees to reach a path junction, where path 8b to Colfosco is signposted downhill to the right. This is steep and precipitous in the winter and is not recommended, so continue straight on along path 8.

Reach another idyllic open clearing dotted with huts and dominated by a sleep slope directly in front. Ascend this on the left where the gradient is easier then cut back right to reach the ski piste and **Rifugio Forcelles** at the top of the hill.

Continue past the rifugio and descend down the left side of the piste. This is quite steep and has the added risk factor of errant skiers, so take care. Reach the bowl of the Val Stella Alpina and follow the more gentle piste right towards the valley, aiming for the cluster of houses just below the gondola leading up to Col Pradat, taking care when crossing the piste. Just below the lift a small road signs path 4 to Colfosco. Descend this steeply entering into the village of **Colfosco**, continuing for 400 metres to reach the idyllic village **church**.

COLFOSCO CHURCH

The beautiful Gothic Colfosco church is dedicated to Saint Vigilius of Trent, the patron saint and first bishop of the town of Trento. Until the 15th century, Colfosco was part of the parish of Laion, a village in the Val Gardena, and as such churchgoers would make the long journey over the Puez and along the Vallunga valley in order to go to mass and bury their dead. It was finally united with Corvara in 1928.

The church is particularly attractive for its picturesque location below the dramatic Val Mesdì, although the interior is also well worth a look, featuring a 19th-century altar crafted by Johann Valentin of Badia and an 18th-century painting of the Virgin Mary. The church also once housed a statue of Saint Virgilius, but this was removed to protect it and has since been replaced by a replica.

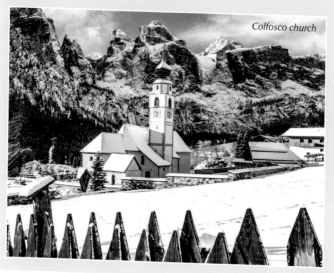

Colfosco church

From here take path 10 to Corvara signed along the road. Passing the fire station on its right, continue downhill for 60 metres then turn left onto another road below a wooden bridge, following signs to Corvara and Pescosta.

This leads briefly downhill then ascends for 50 metres to another sign. Follow this down a small road then traverse the side of the hill overlooking the village. Pass between two houses then follow the road downhill, making a series of switchbacks to reach the hamlet of **Pescosta**. Join another road 100 metres before **Hotel Sassongher** then leave path 10 to descend downhill towards the village to the bridge. Cross this then turn right onto a path, following this for 250 metres to reach the main road. From here continue back to the car park.

Other possibilities

For a shorter itinerary it is possible to park at the top of Colfosco and take the Plans-Frara gondola straight away, removing the walk from and back to Corvara and reducing the itinerary by around 1hr.

ROUTE 18
Santa Croce and Ranch da Andrè

Start	Sas dla Crusc chairlift top station (2040m)
Finish	Badia Abtei (1330m)
Distance	9km
Total ascent	50m
Total descent	760m
Grade	E 1.3
Time	3–4hrs
Aspect of ascent	W
Aspect of descent	W
Map	Tabacco No 07
Parking	Santa Croce lift car park: 46.60942, 11.89623

This excellent route has the added advantage of a chairlift ascent, and the idyllic Ranch da Andrè is the perfect destination for this scenically stunning yet technically straightforward snowshoe below the steep grandeur of the Fanes.

APPROACH

From Corvara in Badia, take the SR244 north, following the Val Badia for 8km to reach Badia Abtei. On entering the village, just before the village square turn right, following signs for the Santa Croce and Sas dla Crusc chairlifts. Park in the ample lift station car park. Take the Santa Croce and Sas dla Crusc chairlifts – the lift station sells single tickets for the two stages.

From the top of the second lift, turn right then after 20 metres follow a track steeply left for 50 metres through the trees to reach the idyllic church of Santa Croce adjacent to **Rifugio Sass dla Crusc**. Walk along the left side of the church and aim for a collection of signposts. Take path 15, signed for Armentara, which leads left just before an old farm building, and follow this to begin contouring below the face. This undulates gently then, after 5mins, crosses between two small huts and continues for 35 metres to another hut with numerous waymarks. Here continue along the main track for 80 metres to a fork, where path 15 leads steeply right. Keep left here and crest a small hill by a bench before descending left for 80 metres to reach a cluster of three ramshackle huts.

Follow the path as it contours right across the hillside, heading due north and entering into the trees. In another 5mins the path makes a sharp bend left (don't be tempted to continue straight on) and then zigzags down for 200 metres to where the trees begin to open out. Follow a blunt ridge down through the trees

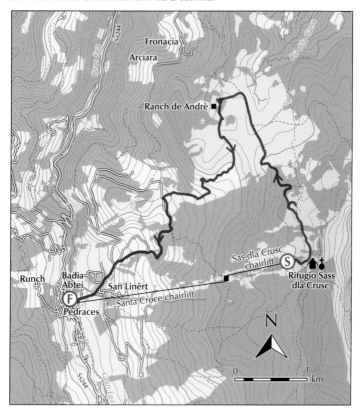

then after another 100 metres reach a clearing with a picnic bench on the left. The scenery is more open now, with wide snowy meadows dotted with picturesque wooden huts. Continue down towards the huts, passing between them to reach a track (usually pisted) which crosses the path by a signpost. Continue straight on, following path 15a to La Val and Wengen. Here, the more adventurous option is to cut directly up to a copse of trees, ascending steeply to reach the traditional farmhouse of **Ranch da Andrè**. Otherwise, continue straight ahead along the pisted track, bearing left (west) and then in another 60 metres turning left to aim for the trees on the crest of the hill where the fence surrounding the Ranch is just visible. Ascend towards this for 5mins – there are often a number of cross country ski pistes here, so avoid treading in the loipers where possible – to reach Ranch da Andrè.

From the hut and facing east, take the uphill path which leads alongside the fence to join a large pisted track (again, take care of the loipers) which leads through the trees then after 100 metres reaches another wooden hut. Continue left of the hut, then in another 100 metres ignore the path branching off right and continue straight on, now walking due south. Continue towards a cluster of huts, pass them on the right side then follow a shallow valley logically for 10mins to where the path bears right, passing between two huts. Follow the track as it bears right (west), passing just right of another hut. There is a good viewpoint overlooking the Val Badia just off the path on the left by a lone tree.

Follow the path to the right of the tree then continue along more open hillside, descending towards the huts below. Stay on the large path to reach a fenced area; enter this and turn left onto another well-worn track to aim for the road at a point by a white farmhouse flanked by a couple of wooden out buildings.

At the road, turn left and continue downhill, following signs for Badia Abtei. Shortly afterwards two cross country ski tracks lead right; continue straight on here and bear left slightly for 50 metres to reach a large sign on a tree, signposted towards Valgiarei-Badia. There is another, more official sign just beyond this, now signing route 'AT' to Badia. This leads to the left of a crest and descends to its left, with excellent views of the Fanes opening out in front. After 500 metres cross a cattle grid (this can be hard to spot in heavy snow) then turn right to descend

The beautiful and iconic church of Santa Croce

a bank and reach a large pisted footpath (often icy). Here follow the signpost for Badia Abtei, which points right on path 7a. This soon enters the trees then descends for 10mins to reach a junction; continue straight on, still following for Badia Abtei.

Join another road and turn left, following this for 300 metres to enter back into the village of **Badia**. Continue easily for another 10mins along the main village road to return back to the lift station.

Other possibilities

This route is equally good done in reverse, providing a more physically challenging alternative with more ascent before taking the chairlifts down.

ROUTE 19
Lech dla Lunch to Lech da Sompont

Start/Finish	Badia Abtei (1330m)
Distance	7km
Total ascent	225m
Total descent	225m
Grade	E
Time	2–3hrs
Aspect of ascent	E
Aspect of descent	E
Map	Tabacco No 07
Parking	Badia Abtei village centre car park: 46.60987, 11.89413

This snowshoe takes place in dense but beautiful forest, making it an ideal choice in poor visibility or on heavy snow days. The route incorporates the fantastically situated Lech da Sompont, which is a great spot for a drink or to try your hand at curling or skating.

APPROACH

From San Martino in Badia take the SS244 south for 10km to reach Badia Abtei. Park in the centre of the village on the left.

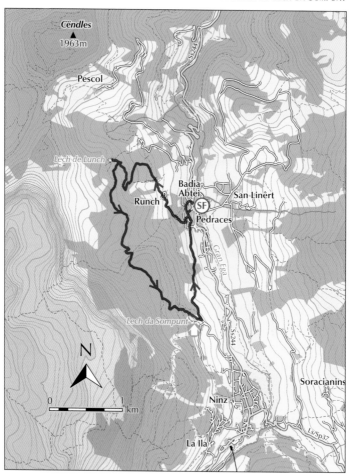

From the centre of **Badia Abtei** cross the road towards Monte Puez, following the road sign to Ciaminades/Runch and a walking sign marking Utia de Puez on path 1. This road ascends steeply and bears around to the left as it levels out. Ignore further signs for path 1 here and continue ascending along the road, picking up signs for path 5 signed to Lech da Sompont, Utia di Gardenaccia and Tru de Lech.

Shortly after the paths split, with path 5 leading up and left. Ignore this and continue following for Lech dla Lunch and Tru de Lech. Continue past a sign marking the end of the Badia village and 30 metres on pass Ciasa Urban – keep straight on here to enter into the woods.

Shortly after entering the woods a sign points left to Utia de Puez on path 1; ignore this and follow the road signed for Lech dla Lunch and Tru de Lech, shortly entering the hamlet of **Runch**. Cross through the buildings, passing a concrete water trough, and continue left up the road. Pass the right side of a wooden barn to reach another sign for 5B Lech dla Lunch/Tru de Lech and follow this, taking in stunning views of the Fanes group.

At the T-junction shortly afterwards turn right, keeping on the 5B. Pass a bench and a wooden 'Strada Privata' sign and continue straight on, following the track through a gate onto the edge of a wooded area. The 5B turns left here to Lech dla Lunch; instead, continue straight on and enter into the woods, following signs for Lech dla Lunch/Tru de Lech. This path has no number but is regularly marked with red and white waymarks on the trees. After 150 metres come to a T-junction with path 1B to Pescol on the right – keep left here, again with no number but frequent waymarks.

After a wooden barrier the path begins to ascend, staying on the large track to reach a junction 10mins on. This is where the smaller path 5B intersects – in heavy snow this shortcut can be hard work, so it is advisable to keep following the larger track which shortly rejoins path 5B.

As the track ascends the trees begin to thin, providing good views of the Puez and Gardenaccia mountains, before reaching a small clearing with a circular fence and a concrete water bunker. Here a path leads off left to Lech da Sompont

130

Enjoying the tranquil woodland surrounding Lech dla Lunch

– this will be taken after visiting the first lake. Continue straight on for 50 metres to reach **Lech dla Lunch**. The lake is not always easily visible with deep snow cover but is an attractive and idyllic winter setting with good views. Double back for the junction and turn right, following signs for Lago di Sompont. The paths are smaller now and harder to spot in heavy snow and without tracks, but keep an eye out for the waymarks painted quite high on the trees. Follow the path as it traverses the hillside, ascending gently then descending to reach a clearing. Pass through the clearing and back into the woods, descending and then levelling out for 10mins. The woodland, gorse and trees make for a veritable winter wonderland, particularly when it's snowing. After bending left, the path makes a sharp right – be careful not to descend left here and look for arrows pointing right, almost doubling back on yourself. Before long the path bears back left and is well signed before ascending more steeply up a short hill.

After the steep section bear left and then in 100 metres join a large track, marked path 1. Continue straight across this to the steeper path marked Lech da Sompont and Tru de Lech, with an old wooden sign pointing to Col Ciaminades and Sompont C. This is the steepest part of the route and is less well marked, but the route is logical and develops in a southwesterly direction. Ascend the steep hill for 250 metres to where it levels out, then continue until the track descends to reach a sign pointing **Lech da Sompont** and Tru de Lech to the left. Turn left and descend steeply to reach the lake.

Lech da Sompont is larger than Lech dla Lunch and is the ideal spot for some traditional winter sports – when the ice is fully frozen it is possible to hire skates and curling stones from the hotel next to the lake, which also serves an excellent hot chocolate.

Leave the lake and head towards the bridge where the ski piste crosses the road, then pick up path 5 to the left, signed Badia Abtei and Tru de Lech. Follow this for 20mins to return to the village of Badia and follow the road back down to the village square and the car.

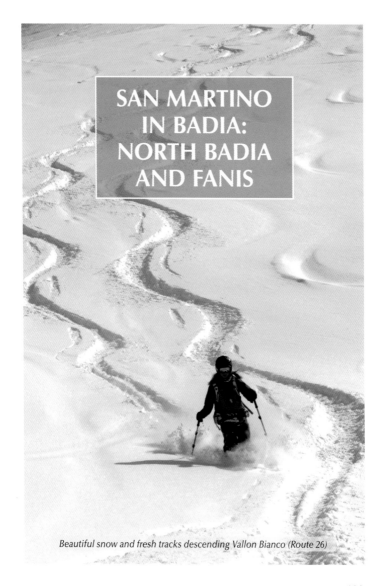

SAN MARTINO IN BADIA: NORTH BADIA AND FANIS

Beautiful snow and fresh tracks descending Vallon Bianco (Route 26)

INTRODUCTION

In terms of local culture the village of San Martino in Badia is particularly interesting with the medieval castle of Ćiastel de Tor playing host to the Micurà de Rü Ladin Institute and Museum. Ladin is a Rhaeto-Romance language that was once widely spoken in mountain communities between Switzerland and the Julian Alps during the Middle Ages. Although only pockets of the language remain, the closely related dialect of Romansch has gained recognition as an official language in Switzerland, while in Italy Ladin continues to be widely spoken in the Dolomite provinces of the South Tyrol and Trentino, where it is recognised as a language by local and national law. Although there are numerous regional variations of the dialect, most Ladin speakers can understand each other and despite the geographical distance even Swiss Romansch still bears remarkable similarities.

Located just off the SS244 at the north side of the Val Badia, San Martino in Badia makes an excellent base for a number of routes in this guide. It is ideally suited to a winter destination, located a short distance from the Plan de Corones ski area, with ski buses bringing the more famous Sella Ronda network into easy reach. Thanks to the slightly more isolated location, winter walks, snowshoes and ski tours unfold in pristinely unspoilt natural landscapes, while the gentle nature of the slopes means that many of the routes can be enjoyed on snowshoes and skis alike.

Many of the routes described here begin from Rifugio Pederù, a large alpine guest house located at the end of the Val Rudo and accessed from San Vigilio di Marebbe. The idyllic valleys of the Fanes-Sennes-Braies natural park are very popular with the locals, although it is rare to hear another English voice. The ski tours and snowshoe routes here are characterised by long, gentle ascents up wide slopes, culminating in excellent views and often rewarded by an apple strudel and a *vin brulé* (Italian for mulled wine) at Rifugio Lavarella or Rifugio Fanes along the way.

San Martino, San Vigilio di Marebbe, La Val and Badia are all well-located for the routes in this itinerary, although San Vigilio is more isolated in terms of accessing other areas included in the guide.

For Routes 24–26, Rifugios Fanes and Lavarella can be used as overnight bases for the tours, saving the two hour approach from Pedaru.

ROUTE 20
Monte Muro

Start/Finish	Pe de Börz (1820m)
Distance	13km
Total ascent	650m
Total descent	650m
Grade	E 2.1
Time	5–6hrs
Aspect of ascent	S
Aspect of descent	N/S
Map	Tabacco No 07
Parking	Pe de Börz car park: 46.68165, 11.82294

This is a long and demanding snowshoe to the solitary summit of Monte Muro (2332m), right on the northern edge of the Dolomites. The peak provides spectacular views over the nearby Sass de Putia (2875m) and on a clear day the Grossglockner (3798m), Grossvenediger (3666m) and high mountains of Austria can be admired. The complete circuit requires good fitness, although it is possible to do an out-and-back trip to the peak via Rifugio Monte Muro (Maurerberghütte), which shortens the day and removes the slightly awkward traverse at the end.

APPROACH

The route starts from the Pe de Börz parking area, 1km before the top of the Passo delle Erbe, just west of Antermoia. From San Martino in Badia take the SP29 west following signs for Passo delle Erbe for 13km, passing through the village of Antermoia and parking at Pe de Börz on a large hairpin turn to the left. The parking area can be identified by a number of information boards, a bus stop on the right and signs for path 1.

The Passo delle Erbe is often signed as closed during the winter months, however usually this restriction only applies to the west side and the parking area can usually still be accessed from Antermoia.

From the parking area follow signs for path 1 towards Rifugio Monte Muro on a pisted track for 80 metres before turning left onto path 2, signposted to Utia Pecol. This leads steeply up through the trees and although the route is seldom tracked it is easily identified by numerous path markers painted on the trees. After 10mins the trees thin and the path reaches a blunt ridgeline. Turn right here, following the depression of a summer vehicle track, which leads east. This descends into an open area dotted with a couple of small wooden huts. Turn left and follow a large signpost for Utia Pecol on path 2, which leads uphill through the trees on a large vehicle track before levelling out and undulating to reach **Utia Pecol** (1930m), 15mins later.

Turn right just past the rifugio, still following signs for path 2 and aiming for a wooden 'ciao' arch, which can be seen to the northeast. Pass through the arch and head towards another path marker up to the right, from where a rightwards traverse leads to another open area with fantastic views of the Fanis Massif and Sass de Putia. Here take path 2b signposted towards Monte Muro, which leads steeply uphill for 100 metres, then turn left following another vehicle track which leads to another beautiful wooden hut after 5mins. Follow path markers leading left into the trees to shortly arrive at a large open area beneath Monte Muro. Here follow any number of lines (there are summer path markers on short wooden stakes but these are often buried when there is a good snow base) to ascend the open slopes, trending slowly rightwards and aiming for ever higher ground to

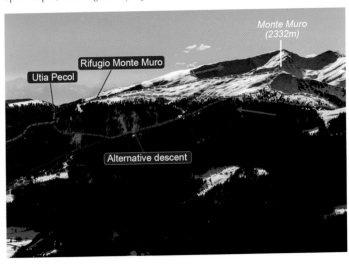

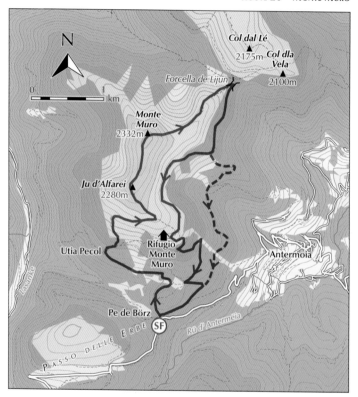

reach the summit of **Monte Muro** (easily identified by a huge wooden cross) in 45mins.

Descend east and then northeast along the ridgeline, following the natural topography and signposting for Forcella de Lijun along path 1A. Descend for 25mins, until the obvious saddle of Forcella de Lijun comes into view, easily identified by a large cross and a shrine. At **Forcella de Lijun**, turn right and follow signposting for path 1 following a larger track south as it leads uphill through the forest for 25mins to reach a junction with path 20a. Path 20a continues down the valley and offers an alternative route back, see Other possibilities below.

Turn on to path 1, which soon exits from the trees to begin a long traverse, staying just above the treeline (this can be hard work in icy snow) and aiming for

137

Passing two of the many beautiful huts with views of Sass de Putia

the ridge just south of Monte Muro. Reach the ridge and descend easily to the superbly situated **Rifugio Monte Muro** to join a pisted track. From here follow good signposting for Pe de Börz to return to the car in 15mins.

Other possibilities

If the traverse isn't safe, another option is to continue descending on path 20a for a short distance before turning south and following a vehicle track through the forest to join onto path 1 just above the car park. It isn't signposted and goes through forest so good navigation is required.

Another option, from the summit of **Monte Muro**, is to return by descending back down the ridge before following it south and then southeast to **Rifugio Monte Muro** and the pisted track of path 1 which leads easily back to the car (1hr).

ROUTE 21
Crep dales Dodesc

Start/Finish	Longiarù outskirts (1500m)
Distance	11km
Total ascent	850m
Total descent	850m
Grade	E 2.2
Time	4–5hrs
Aspect of ascent	S
Aspect of descent	S/N
Map	Tabacco No 07
Equipment	Crampons, ice axe, harness and rope required for the alterntive descent of Antersas North Couloir (4.1)
Parking	Car park on outskirts of Longiarù: 46.63179, 11.84905

This long tour explores a remote part of the Puez Odle group, ascending the beautiful Val D'Antersas between the dramatic rock walls of Ciampani and Somplunt and culminating in the spectacular summit of Crep dales Dodesc, which offers dramatic views in every direction. The descent offers the option of skiing back down your uphill tracks (often with excellent snow), or an alternative option is to descend the impressive north couloir of Antersas, which requires good ski mountaineering experience. The final uphill stage of the route takes a series of south facing slopes which require a stable snowpack, suitable weather conditions and correct temperatures for a safe ascent.

APPROACH

The route departs from just south west of Longiarù, a small and remote village under the dramatic flanks of Sass de Putia (Peitlerkofel) (2875m). From San Martino in Badia follow the SP29 west for 300 metres and then take the SP57 signposted on the left to Longiarù just before the first hairpin of the Passo delle Erbe. Follow the road for 5km, passing through Longiarù itself, until the road swings sharply to the right with clear signs for the parking area, located 200 metres up the road on the left.

Exit the car park and follow the road you drove in on for 300 metres until reaching a T junction. Turn right and follow the road until it ends, ignoring path 6 which turns off to the left, where a signpost indicates the start of path 9, signposted towards Antersas. Put skins on and follow the track for 25mins first ascending and then gradually descending, ignoring two unsignposted turn offs to the right and reaching a signpost pointing Pedraces to the left and Antersas to the right. Turn right and head steeply uphill through the woods, taking care to follow the sporadic path markers on the trees until joining with path 6 in 40mins. Turn right onto this to ascend a large summer vehicle track up the valley, eventually reaching a fence with a gate where the vehicle track ends.

Pass through the gate to reach the first view of the **Val D'Antersas** proper. The summer path leads up on the right, contouring around the bowl in front. However if the conditions are not stable enough to traverse the bowl it is better to drop down slightly into the valley and then kick turn back up the opposite side. Follow the path or the bottom of the valley as required, leaving the treeline behind for

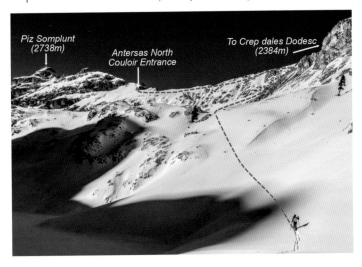

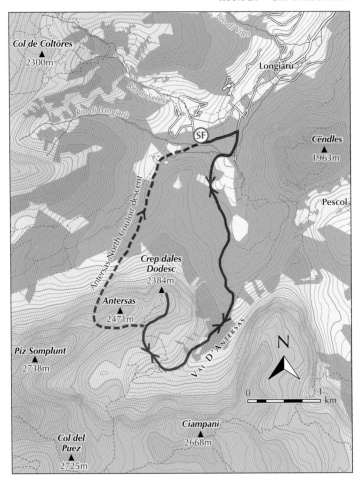

40mins until reaching a characteristic and rather beautiful tree in the centre of a valley with a shrine and a nearby signpost.

Turn right and follow path 12 signposted to Crep dales Dodesc, making a rising traverse leftwards and aiming to the right of Piz Somplunt. Skirt another bowl on the left, traversing beneath the rock cliffs on the right before open slopes

Leaving the trees behind and entering into the Val D'Antersas

lead back right towards **Crep dales Dodesc**. The summit is easily identified by a very large wooden cross on a broad shoulder and provides spectacular views in all directions.

To descend, ski down your uphill tracks (it is possible to do a small loop lower down by staying on the large track of path 6, removing the narrow section through the woods on path 9).

Other possibilities

For a suitably experienced party it is possible to ski down the Antersas North Couloir (4.1). From the summit of **Crep dales Dodesc**, keeping skins on, ski down for 40 metres or so and then traverse under the Antersas ridgeline, heading towards Piz Somplunt on a broad shoulder to reach the couloir on the right by an evident saddle before the rock steps of Piz Somplunt. There are two entrances, although the upper entrance which provides a view down the length of the couloir is generally preferable. After a period of strong wind there may be a large cornice present at the entrance, necessitating the need to either chop through it or abseil in. The first few metres are narrow and difficult until passing through a bottleneck to gain the main couloir. From here the skiing is often superb on powder snow and leads all the way down to the valley floor. From here, join a pisted track which leads downhill all the way back to the car park.

There are a number of difficult north facing colours on **Piz Somplunt** that offer challenging gully descents for skiers with appropriate experience.

ROUTE 22
Munt da Medalges

Start/Finish	Longiarù outskirts (1500m)
Distance	11km
Total ascent	900m
Total descent	900m
Grade	E 1.3
Time	4–5hrs
Aspect of ascent	E
Aspect of descent	E
Map	Tabacco No 07
Parking	Car park on outskirts of Longiarù: 46.63179, 11.84905

This much frequented ski tour does not involve any major difficulties and often offers fantastic snow due to its north facing aspect. The full tour up to the summit of Medalges (2454m) is long but the out-and-back nature of the route means you can turn around when you wish.

APPROACH

The route departs from just south west of Longiarù, a small and remote village in the Val Badia under the dramatic flanks of Sass de Putia (Peitlerkofel) (2875m). From San Martino in Badia follow the SP29 west for 300 metres and then take the SP57 signposted on the left to Longiarù just before the first hairpin of the Passo delle Erbe. Follow the road for 5km, passing through Longiarù itself, until the road swings sharply to the right with clear signs for the parking area. The car park is located 200 metres up the road on the left.

From the car park follow signs for path 5, which leads west out of the top of the car park along a pisted track. Follow this for 15mins, ignoring the turn off to the right for path 5b and continuing until a large boulder, where path 5 is signed off to the right. Take this, leaving the main track and following the path up into the woodlands, getting progressively steeper. Reach a large arrow and follow this

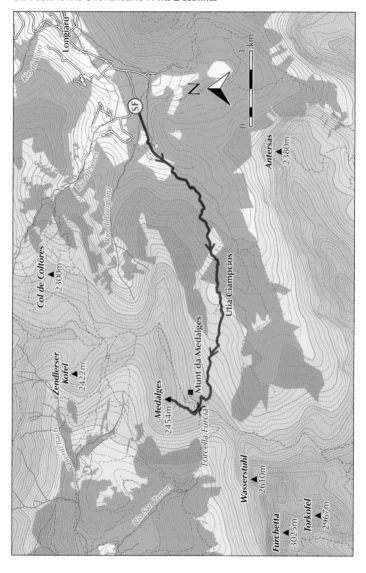

onto a single track. A further 15mins of ascent leads out into an open area adjacent to several idyllic wooden huts and some fantastic views.

Approaching the Medalges farmhouse with views of Piz Somplunt

Continue uphill and pass to the right of **Utia Ciampcios**, following the blunt ridgeline between the two valleys and heading west to reach an open slope. Continue ascending this to the west on slightly steeper ground to reach the **Munt da Medalges farmhouse** in a further 15mins. The nearby Forcella Furcia is easily identified by a large shrine in the centre of the col directly above you. From here you can either ascend steeply to the col or make a long but easier traverse to the right before turning back left to join the ridgeline just above **Forcella Furcia**. Once you have enjoyed the stunning views down into the Val di Funes below, make a right (north) and ascend up the ridgeline to the summit of **Medalges** (2454m).

To begin the descent, ski down your uphill tracks as far as the Munt da Medalges farmhouse. From here many lines are possible: either continue to descend in the line of your uphill tracks, sticking to the ridgeline ascended on the way up, or alternatively drop into the valley to the southeast, eventually joining the pisted track that serves as a toboggan run in the winter and follow this back to the car park.

ROUTE 23
Malga Vaciara

Start/Finish	Longiarù (1430m)
Distance	12km
Total ascent	800m
Total descent	800m
Grade	E
Time	5–6hrs
Aspect of ascent	S
Aspect of descent	S
Map	Tabacco No 07
Parking	Car park in centre of Longiarù: 46.64076, 11.86144

Without doubt one of the best snowshoe routes in the area, this is a hard but superb itinerary offering stunning views of Sass de Putia and the Puez and Fanis massifs. The route starts in the Val di Morins (Valley of the Mills) and culminates in an open air mountain museum, where various sculptures add significant cultural interest to what is already an outstanding route. Parts of the itinerary are steep and as such the route requires an absolutely safe snowpack and a fit party.

APPROACH

The route departs from Longiarù, a small and remote village below the dramatic flanks of Sass de Putia (Peitlerkofel) (2875m). From San Martino in Badia follow the SP29 west for 300 metres before turning left onto the SP57 towards Longiarù, just before the first hairpin of the Passo delle Erbe. Follow the road for 5km to reach the large church in the centre of Longiarù itself. Continue past the church for 100 metres and park in the car park on the left.

From the car park, continue up the road in a southwesterly direction for 100 metres then turn right onto path 4, signposted towards the Val di Morins. Continue southwest, aiming for the top right corner of the field to enter into trees near a small cluster of houses. Follow another signpost for path 4, entering into the next field and passing to the right side of the middle one of three huts, aiming for a shrine. At the shrine bear right and ascend more steeply towards a large white building, Lüch de Vanc, identified by a wooden hexagonal summerhouse. Pass in front of **Lüch de Vanc** to turn left onto a road. Follow the road downhill for 50 metres until reaching a bridge; turn right here, leaving the road and following path 4 signposted to Sass de Putia and the Val di Morins.

Piccolo Sass de Putia (2813)

Sass de Putia (2875m)

Malga Vaciara

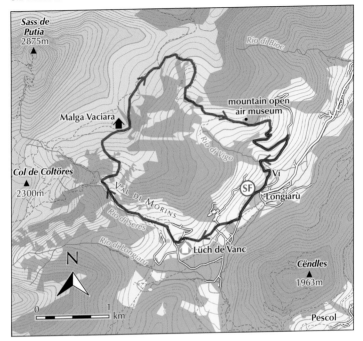

Ascend the valley, following the right-hand side of the stream.

There is an interesting **detour** here, which takes the left side of the stream to visit a number of charming mills. Follow signs for the Morins to then cross back over to the right side of the stream to rejoin the main route. From here the couloir of Antersas (Route 21) can be observed to the south.

Continue for another 10mins to reach a signpost for path 4. Follow sporadic waymarks uphill, many of which can get buried in the snow and so hard to spot, to ascend a steep vehicle track. Cross a bridge then ascend steeply between two streams in the centre of the valley. Shortly after reach a sign for the natural park where path 4 turns left; keep right here, following a vehicle track signed to Malga Vaciara.

Cross the stream and make a rising traverse to the right, crossing through an area of boulders to reach the trees. Follow the track briefly through the woods to reach another open area just below a wooden hut. Traverse rightwards across this slope to reach another cluster of trees. Don't enter into these and instead go steeply uphill; this is hard work and it can be worth clipping the back of the snowshoes down kicking steps. Continue up the slope, passing to the left-hand side of a large boulder.

Some 5mins after the boulder reach a wooden hut with a painted waymark; pass this on the right side then before the next open slope, trend left to reach an old signpost for Malga Vaciara some 40 metres after the hut. It is well worth looking back here to take in the superb views of Crep dales Dodesc (Route 21), Antersas and Piz Somplunt. Continue for another 100 metres to reach another signpost pointing up the slope towards a large buttress. Head towards this, picking the best line depending on the snow conditions. After 70 metres reach another sign and turn right towards the rifugio.

This leads into a traverse below the steeper slope, passing another wooden hut and reaching some trees on the right side. Here turn back on yourself to make a rising traverse across the steep slope, aiming for the lowest area. This requires safe snow conditions but the summer path can be made out under the snow, assisting in navigation. It is also possible to traverse left (west) all the way beneath the face, adding an additional 40mins.

Continue to reach a signpost at the top of the slope, from where the gradient eases and opens out into the large plateau below Sass de Putia, offering excellent

Superb views from underneath Sass de Putia towards Crep dales Dodesc and the Puez Group

views. After a well-earned pause, continue to ascend towards the hut on the right before traversing easier ground, still following signs towards Malga Vaciara. Reach a track where the waymark of path 35 can sometimes be made out through the snow and descend this into the trees, circumnavigating a small buttress on the left. Continue to follow the track as it veers north and leads into easier and more open terrain, again with stunning views.

After a further 15mins round a corner to reach 'Roda de Putia' and the first glimpse of **Malga Vaciara**. Continue towards this, passing above it and continuing the traverse around another small corner. Here begin to descend slightly, aiming for two wooden huts by a shrine. Follow the path as it bends back right and descends for 30 metres before turning sharply left to pass above another pair of huts. The track then weaves down the mountain and is poorly signed but logical.

At a sharp hairpin to the left, don't be tempted to follow the path leading uphill on the right and instead follow the track into the start of the **mountain open air museum**. Continue through the museum, passing an assortment of sculptures and artefacts ranging from the sublime to the ridiculous, until reaching the hamlet of **Vi** in 40mins. Follow the road and waymarks for path 9 for a further 25mins to reach the car park and the church.

Other possibilities
It is possible to follow the initial part of this itinerary up to the large plateau of Piccolo Sass de Putia (3.1), taking about 4hrs there and back.

ROUTE 24
Utia Lavarella circuit

Start/Finish	Pederù (1550m)
Distance	13km
Total ascent	500m
Total descent	500m
Grade	E 1.3
Time	4–5hrs
Aspect of ascent	N/S
Aspect of descent	S/N
Map	Tabacco No 03/07
Parking	Rifugio Pederù car park: 46.63824, 12.0416

This beautiful circuit ventures into the vast lunar landscape that makes up the huge plateau to the west of Utia Lavarella, providing an unusual glimpse of the Fanis peaks from a seldom-frequented winter perspective.

APPROACH

The route begins from Rifugio Pederù at the head of the Valle de Rudo. From San Martino in Badia drive north on the SS244 for 6km to reach the village of Longega. Here turn right, following signs for San Vigilio. Turn left in the centre of San Vigilio and then almost immediately back right, following signs for Pederù. Drive down the Valle de Rudo for 11km until the road ends at the car park by Rifugio Pederù.

From the rifugio, follow the large pisted track that leads south and is clearly sign-posted towards Rifugio Lavarella and Rifugio Fanes. Beware as the track is often used by tobogganists, ski tourers and snowmobiles all moving at high speed! Follow the track uphill for 2hrs, with a number of optional 'shortcuts' which skip the switchbacks, to reach a prominent junction with Rifugio Lavarella signposted to the right and Rifugio Fanes signposted straight ahead. Turn right following for Rifugio Lavarella along a pisted track to reach the rifugio in 600 metres.

Sasso delle Dieci (3026m)

Sasso delle Nove (2968m)

Rifugio Lavarella

Rifugio Fanes

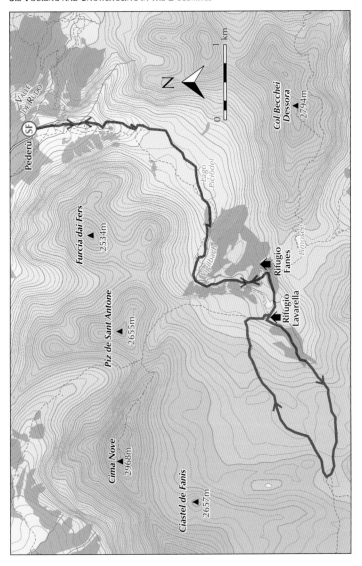

A group returning towards Rifugio Fanes

Pass the **Rifugio Lavarella** on its right side and enter into an area of sparse trees, heading southwest towards a long cliff. Contour below this and keep to the area of thinner vegetation. Pass the cliff and ascend a steeper section, staying to the left of a rocky outcrop. Skirt this and when the terrain allows turn right (northeast), descending and then traversing a large open area above the long rocky cliff. Pass above the cliff and then begin to descend following the natural topography, passing above the last significant cliff. It is possible to turn right here and descend more steeply to return to Rifugio Lavarella. Continue east now, picking the best route (many possible variations) to enter back into sparse trees and a shallow valley which leads back onto the pisted track just before the junction between paths 7 and 11.

If you wish to visit **Rifugio Fanes** for refreshments, turn right and walk easily for 5mins to reach the hut. To return, follow your uphill tracks back to the car park.

Other possibilities

The large plateau surrounding Rifugio Lavarella allows for many possible lines and variations to the surrounding peaks, depending on how far you wish to go.

To significantly shorten the route it is possible to arrange a snowmobile ride from Pederù with either Rifugio Lavarella or Rifugio Fanes (this must be booked in advance).

ROUTE 25
Col Becchei Dessora

Start/Finish	Pederù (1550m)
Distance	15km
Total ascent	800m
Total descent	800m
Grade	F
Time	4–5hrs
Aspect of ascent	S/W
Aspect of descent	W/S
Map	Tabacco No 03/07
Parking	Rifugio Pederù car park: 46.63824, 12.0416

This is an exceptionally popular ski touring itinerary throughout the season as it gains a beautifully panoramic summit in a dramatic and remote environment without presenting any major technical difficulties.

APPROACH

The tour begins from Rifugio Pederù at the head of the Valle de Rudo. From San Martino in Badia drive north on the SS244 for 6km until reaching the village of Longega and turn right here, following for San Vigilio. Turn left in the centre of San Vigilio and then almost immediately back right following signs for Pederù. Drive down the Valle de Rudo for 11km until the road ends at the car park by Rifugio Pederù.

From the rifugio follow the large pisted track that leads south clearly signposted towards Rifugio Lavarella and Rifugio Fanes. Beware as the track is often used by tobogganists, ski tourers and snowmobiles all moving at high speed! Follow the track uphill for 2hrs, with a number of optional 'shortcuts' which skip the switchbacks, to reach a prominent junction with Rifugio Lavarella signposted to the right and Rifugio Fanes signposted straight ahead. Follow for **Rifugio Fanes**. This is located a further 200 metres up the track and is open during winter peak

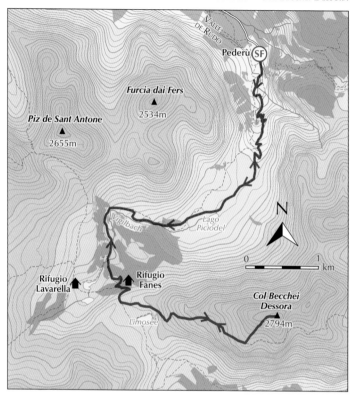

season, providing an excellent spot for a rest. Pass the rifugio, keeping it on the left and continuing uphill to a smaller building at the back of the hut. Begin to make a series of switchbacks uphill following the summer paths 10 and 11. The well-tracked path soon leads up onto a large open plateau dominated by a large cross, offering superb views of Monte Castello straight on, Lavarella, Conturines and the Messner slabs around to the right and the objective of Col Becchei to the left. From this point in good visibility the rest of the route is easily visible to the east and often tracks can be seen leading up the valley to a shoulder and then left to the summit.

Stay to the right of the line of cliffs, following an obvious ramp and taking a logical line to a broader shoulder with the foundations of a wooden hut

Enjoying the south facing aspect in good snow

just visible beneath the snow and a sign on a wooden stake pointing left to Col Becchei. There are two saddles visible, the first shoulder forming the false summit and the second the true summit marked with a cross on the right. Continue more steeply now, making kick turns up the shoulder to reach a broad summit ridge. Follow this to the summit cross on **Col Becchei Dessora** (2794m), reached in about an hour from the plateau. There are now great views towards Cortina, Antelao, the Cristallo and Sorapis groups and the rear sides of the three Tofanas.

To descend, reverse the route.

Other possibilities

To significantly shorten the route it is possible to arrange a snowmobile ride from Pederù with either Rifugio Lavarella or Rifugio Fanes (this must be arranged in advance).

ROUTE 26
Monte Castello

Start/Finish	Pederù (1550m)
Distance	18km
Total ascent	750m
Total descent	750m
Grade	E 2.1
Time	5–6hrs
Aspect of ascent	N
Aspect of descent	N
Map	Tabacco No 03/07
Parking	Rifugio Pederù car park: 46.63824, 12.0416

This long, varied and technically easy ski tour can be done throughout the season and nearly always offers good and safe snow due to its gentle gradient and north facing aspect. Although the route doesn't quite reach the summit of Monte Castello (2817m), the saddle to its right offers stunning views over to the three Tofanas and the adjacent Val Travenanzes.

APPROACH

The route begins from Rifugio Pederù at the head of the Valle de Rudo. From San Martino in Badia, drive north on the SS244 for 6km to reach the village of Longega then turn right for San Vigilio. Turn left in the centre of San Vigilio and then almost immediately back right, following signs for Pederù. Drive down the Valle de Rudo for 11km to where the road ends at the car park by Rifugio Pederù.

From the rifugio put skins on and follow the large pisted track that leads south, clearly signposted towards Rifugio Lavarella and Rifugio Fanes. Beware as the track is often used by tobogganists, ski tourers and snowmobiles all moving at high speed! Follow the track uphill for 2hrs, with a number of optional 'short-cuts' which skip the switchbacks, to reach a prominent junction where Rifugio

157

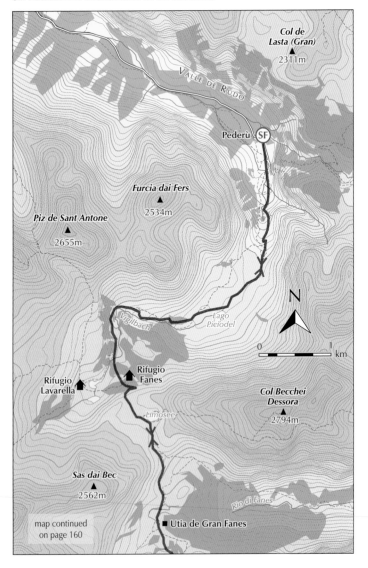

Col de
Lasta (Gran)
▲ 2311m

VALLE DE RUDO

Pederü ⓢⒻ

Furcia dai Fers
▲
2534m

Piz de Sant Antone
▲
2655m

Vilbach

Lago
Piciodel

N

0   1
km

Rifugio
Fanes
▲

Rifugio
Lavarella ▲

Col Becchei
Dessora
▲
2794m

Limosee

Sas dai Bec
▲
2562m

map continued
on page 160

■ Utia de Gran Fanes

Rio di Fanes

Lavarella is signposted to the right and Rifugio Fanes is signposted straight ahead. Follow for **Rifugio Fanes**. This is located a further 200 metres up the track and is open in the winter during peak season, providing an excellent spot for a rest.

Ascending the lower valley from Rifugio Pederù

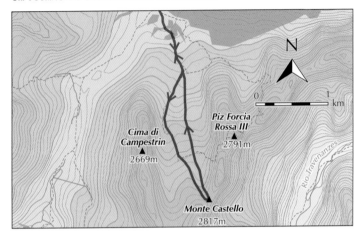

Pass the rifugio, keeping it on the left and continuing uphill to a smaller building at the back of the hut, and begin to make a series of switchbacks uphill following the summer paths 10 and 11. The well-tracked path soon leads up onto a large open plateau dominated by a large cross, offering superb views of Monte Castello straight on, Lavarella, Conturines and the Messner slabs around to the right and Col Becchei Desora (Route 25) to the left.

Continue south, staying on path 11, to quickly reach **Utia de Gran Fanes farmhouse**. Continue past this to enter into an area of sparse trees at the base of Vallon Bianco. From here the valley can be ascended on either the left or right side: an ascent of the right side is recommended simply to make the loop more complete, avoiding the ski fall line from Monte Castello. Ascend towards the cliffs of **Cima di Campestrin**, staying on the left side of a huge boulderfield beneath the face. Now follow the natural valley topography over the next slope to the steeper face beneath **Monte Castello**. Kick turn up this to the right-hand side of the tower, taking in some stunning views to the east.

To descend, ski down directly from Monte Castello, keeping to the east side of the valley and avoiding several rocky drops to rejoin your uphill tracks near to Utia de Gran Fanes farmhouse. Follow these back to the start of the route.

Other possibilities

To significantly shorten the route it is possible to arrange a snowmobile ride from Pederù with either Rifugio Lavarella or Rifugio Fanes (this must be booked in advance).

ARABBA: MARMOLADA AND LIVINALLONGO

Climbing up the final steep section to reach Forcella Marmolada (Route 28)

INTRODUCTION

First tracks up through sparse woodland (Route 29)

At 3343m, the Marmolada is the highest mountain in the Dolomites and it comes as no surprise that some of the best snow conditions for freeride and off-piste skiing are often found down its impressive north face. As these itineraries are not strictly ski tours, requiring little or no uphill gain, they have not been included in this guide. There are, however, a number of excellent local resources available that provide detailed information on the routes (see Appendix E). The Marmolada is also justifiably popular with piste skiers thanks to the 12km red run, which

descends from the top cablecar at Punta Rocca to Malga Ciapela in the valley.

However, freeride and piste skiing isn't all the Marmolada has to offer, and Forcella Marmolada and Punta Penia Spallone are superb technical ski tours. Both require some skill and experience of winter mountaineering for the ascents but reward with superb views and a unique sense of achievement; Punta Penia Spallone exits onto the true summit of the Marmolada, a beautiful and solitary place which is a far cry from the bustling crowds of the

MARMOLADA

Often referred to as the 'Queen of the Dolomites', the broad expanse of the Marmolada consists of a complex chain of peaks that run from east to west, gaining in elevation as they go. At 3343m, Punta Penia is the highest peak in the Dolomites and is much coveted during the summer and winter months by climbers and ski mountaineers alike.

During the summer, the summit of Punta Penia is often accessed via the steel cabling which runs along the West Ridge, representing the only truly alpine via ferrata in the Dolomites. The route was first equipped in 1903 by a local alpine guide, Vincenzo Fersuoch, on behalf of the Nuremburg branch of the German and Austrian Alpine Club, and is often considered the oldest via ferrata in the Dolomites.

The Marmolada takes its name from the ancient Greek word 'maramairo' (to sparkle), no doubt inspired by the white expanse of the Ghiacciaio della Marmolada, the largest glacier in the Dolomites which dominates the northern slopes. The mountain chain played an integral role during the First World War when vast networks of tunnels were carved into the glacier ice by the Austro-Hungarian troops occupying the position. Historians and excavators have since discovered some 12km of tunnels in this veritable 'City of Ice', with chambers large enough to house 300 troops at a time. A war museum is located at the mid station of the Malga Ciapela cablecar, with numerous exhibits detailing and displaying many of the artefacts found in the region.

By contrast the enigmatic and secluded south face of the Marmolada receives very little attention outside of the climbing community. However for those in the know this beautiful 'silver face' boasts over a vertical kilometre of immaculate limestone in the centre and is one of the greatest big walls in the world, drawing climbers from far and wide.

As befits such an iconic symbol and the highest peak in the range, the Marmolada is not without its share of folklore. One of the many tales recounts how, on the 5 August many years ago, the people of the Alpine pastures were celebrating the festival of Madonna della Neve when it began to rain. An old woman left the procession to collect the hay she had left drying in the meadows, saying that she didn't care about the Virgin Mary as long as her hay was dry. At that moment it began to snow, burying the lady and covering the Alpine meadows in a deep white blanket. From that moment the Marmolada Glacier was created, and on clear moonlit nights the old woman's cries can still be heard echoing over the ice.

cablecar station. Although not reaching the summit, Forcella Marmolada provides a characteristic abseil descent before following the open slopes of the Val Contrin, a truly magical and deserted winter environment.

At the base of the Marmolada lies Serrai di Sottoguda, a deep gorge carved between the mountains, which in the winter months is transformed into a veritable ice climbing paradise. Climbers can be seen scaling the numerous ice falls throughout the winter while the annual ice festival held in January is a Mecca for enthusiasts of the sport. For a more sedate way of enjoying the scenery, a footpath leads from Malga Ciapela at the base of the Marmolada to the village of Sottoguda (watch out for skiers snowploughing down the path) from where a bus service links back to the lift system.

Thanks to the Arabba-Marmolada ski area lifts, the village of Arabba is ideally situated for reaching the Marmolada before the crowds from Selva, Corvara and Canazei arrive via the Sella Ronda circuit. Characterised by a somewhat rustic feel compared to the neighbouring villages, it nonetheless has an excellent selection of hotels, garnìs (bed and breakfasts) and holiday apartments and is reasonably well served for restaurants and pizzerias. The pistes of the jagged Portavescovo ridgeline accessed by gondola and cablecar are some of the best in the area, benefiting from a shady north facing aspect and retaining good snow at any stage of the season. The Sella Ronda lifts provide convenient access to the Corvara, Canazei and Selva areas while the Falzarego and Cortina areas are within easy striking distance by road.

There are also some accommodation options in Malga Ciapela at the base of the Marmolada itself but the somewhat isolated location makes this inconvenient for accessing the other areas covered in the guide.

ROUTE 27
Punta Penia

Start	Rifugio Pian dei Fiacconi (2620m)
Finish	Lago di Fedaia (2060m)
Distance	6km
Total ascent	730m
Total descent	1300m
Grade	PD 3.2
Time	4–5hrs
Aspect of ascent	N
Aspect of descent	N
Map	Tabacco No 07
Equipment	Crampons, ice axe
Return to start	Skiers who took the alternative approach (see Approach below) and descended from the cablecar to Rifugio Pian dei Fiacconi will need to rejoin the piste network by taking the bucket lift and making another long traverse back to the ski pistes at the east end of the Lago di Fedaia reservoir. Alternatively, pole back along the track that runs the length of the south side of the reservoir (tiring).
Parking	Pian dei Fiacconi bucket lift car park: 46.45857, 11.86347

This ski tour ascends to the summit of Punta Penia (3343m), the highest point of the Marmolada and the Dolomites. The route is best done during the spring to ensure good snow cover and to avoid icy sections.

APPROACH

The route departs from Rifugio Pian dei Fiacconi, accessed by a bucket lift taken from the west end of Lago di Fedaia. Unfortunately the driving approach via the Passo Fedaia is long, especially as it is often closed on the Canazei (west) side.

From Arabba take the SR48 east for 9km and then make a very sharp right signposted towards Alleghe onto the SS563. Follow the road downhill for 8km to reach a T junction, turning right onto the SP641 following signs for Malga Ciapela. Follow the road for 15km, passing Malga Ciapela to reach Lago di Fedaia. Continue to the far end of the lake then turn left to drive over the dam wall and park at the base of the Pian dei Fiacconi bucket lift.

Alternatively, a base such as Arabba is perfect for this itinerary as it is easy to approach and return using the ski pistes. Take the lift to Portavescovo and follow the piste network to Malga Ciapella. Take the Punta Rocca cable-car to the top and descend (crevasse risk in early and late season) to Rifugio Pian dei Fiacconi, situated at the top of the bucket lift where the route begins.

From the top of the lift make a rising traverse to the west, aiming under the north face of the Marmolada (the largest buttress, Punta Penia). Round this and ascend the valley to the left with many kick turns, aiming for the top right corner where a snow slope breaches the buttress to the right.

Climb up the subsequent snow slope which trends rightwards, often requiring crampons if the snow is icy, to reach the main ridgeline. Turn left here and ascend the large open snow slope in a southeasterly direction, searching for ever higher ground to reach the **Capanna Punta Penia** hut and nearby summit cross. The view

Approaching the summit of Punta Penia (3343m)

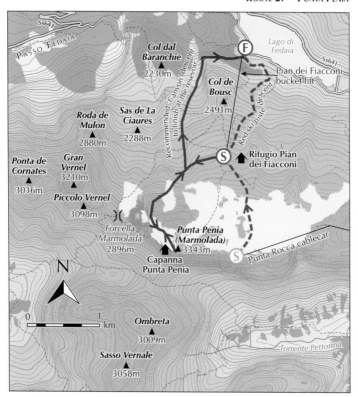

from the roof of the Dolomites is superb in every direction and overlooks nearly every major group of the range on a clear day.

To descend, ski down your uphill tracks until reaching the first buttress passed after the long traverse from the bucket lift. To descend the canyon and finish at the reservoir, ski down the subsequent open slope, keeping to the right and avoiding the cliffs to the left before angling back to the left when the gradient eases. The rift in the rock forming the canyon can now clearly be seen; aim for its uppermost left-hand side, which provides the easiest entrance. Ski through the canyon, which is much easier than first appearances might suggest, to reach another open slope. An easier alternative to the canyon descent is to reverse the route back to the bucket lift and ski the red ski piste back to the Lago di Fedaia.

Ski down the open slope, keeping to the right and aiming for the bottom corner of the large buttress (**Col di Bousc**), entering into sparse vegetation. Round the buttress to begin the traverse back towards Lago di Fedaia. Sidestep up a steeper section then make a long traverse. There are two possible lines here, the summer path and a higher natural line; if in doubt stay high, following the most logical route as per the natural topography. Care needs to be taken as the whole traverse develops above large cliffs and as such requires a safe snowpack and attentive navigation if the way isn't tracked. A final short ski at the end of the traverse leads to the bottom of the **Pian dei Fiacconi bucket lift**.

Other possibilities
For exceptionally fit parties this route can be combined with Forcella Marmolada (Route 28) to create an impressive traverse of the Marmolada group taking around 5–6hrs.

ROUTE 28
Forcella Marmolada

Start	Rifugio Pian dei Fiacconi (2626m)
Finish	Ciampac cablecar parking (1490m)
Distance	11km
Total ascent	300m
Total descent	1440m
Grade	PD 3.1
Time	3–4hrs
Aspect of ascent	N
Aspect of descent	S
Map	Tabacco No 07
Equipment	Rope, crampons, ice axe, mountaineering equipment
Return to start	For those parking at Lago di Fedaia, with sufficient time it is possible to take the Alba/Belvedere cablecar network and ski back to the start with an off-piste descent to return to the reservoir. If the Passo Fedaia is open (this is often closed due to avalanche risk so it is worth asking the local tourist information to confirm) another option is to take a short taxi ride back to the reservoir.
Parking	Pian dei Fiacconi bucket lift car park: 46.45857, 11.86347

This is a beautiful and seldom frequented itinerary that requires mountaineering experience for ascending the final slope to Forcella Marmolada (2896m) and the subsequent abseil into the Valle Rosolia. The initial part of the descent is south facing, necessitating careful timing for a safe yet enjoyable descent.

From the top of the lift traverse west, following signs for path 606 and ferrata, descending a little to pass underneath a large buttress before coming out into a large valley. Forcella Marmolada should be clearly visible from here to the

APPROACH

The route departs from Rifugio Pian dei Fiacconi, accessed by a bucket lift taken from the west end of Lago di Fedaia. Unfortunately the driving approach via the Passo Fedaia is long, especially as it is often closed on the Canazei (west) side.

From Arabba take the SR48 east for 9km and then make a very sharp right signposted towards Alleghe onto the SS563. Follow the road downhill for 8km to reach a T junction, turning right onto the SP641 following for Malga Ciapela. Follow the road for 15km, passing Malga Ciapela and reaching Lago di Fedaia. Continue to the far end of the lake then turn left to drive over the dam wall and park at the base of the Pian dei Fiacconi bucket lift. If approaching by car some thought needs to be given to the logistics of returning from Alba in the Val di Fassa where the tour ends.

Alternatively, a base such as Arabba is perfect for this itinerary as it is easy to approach and return using the ski pistes. Take the lift to Portavescovo and follow the piste network to Malga Ciapella. Take the Punta Rocca cablecar to the top and descend (crevasse risk in early and late season) to Rifugio Pian dei Fiacconi, situated at the top of the bucket lift where the route begins

southwest. Ascend the valley until reaching the steep ground just below the saddle, which often requires the use of crampons for the final 100m or so. This part of the ascent is pictured in the photograph in the section introduction above.

Descending onto the open slope beneath Forcella Marmolada

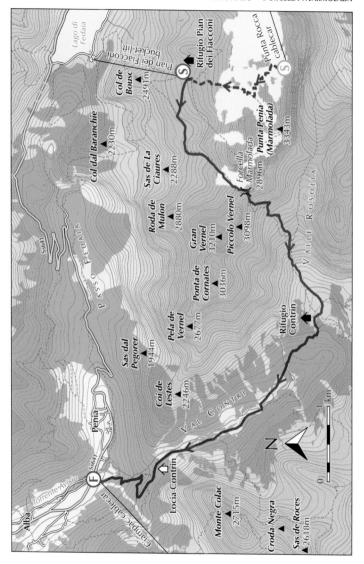

On gaining the saddle of **Forcella Marmolada** the descent couloir can be viewed on the opposite side (adjacent to some metal rungs if these are not buried by the snow). The first steep and narrow section must often be confronted with an abseil (the ferrata wires provide convenient anchors) until the slope widens and the gradient eases.

Ski the initial couloir until this widens then make a long traverse to the left, staying above several large boulders before entering a shallow valley littered with rocks and following the natural line back right to reach **Rifugio Contrin**. From here follow the forestry track (path 602) all the way down the **Val Contrin**, passing several flat sections, which require a good amount of poling. Go through a gate at the end of the valley to shortly arrive at the small **Locia Contrin building**. From here follow the large track down a number of hairpins (beware of people touring up) all the way down to the **Penia – Ciampac cablecar** parking area in the Val di Fassa. If the final track does not have sufficient snow cover for a ski descent it is possible to traverse west through the trees to join the piste leading back to the lifts.

*Forcella Marmolada
(2896m)*

Other possibilities

For exceptionally fit parties this route can be combined with the descent from Punta Penia – Spallone (Route 27) to create an impressive traverse of the Marmolada group taking around 5–6hrs.

ROUTE 29
Monte Sief

Start/Finish	Corte (1600m)
Distance	8km
Total ascent	750m
Total descent	750m
Grade	E 2.1
Time	4–5hrs
Aspect of ascent	N
Aspect of descent	N
Map	Tabacco No 07
Parking	Outskirts of Corte: 46.49705, 11.92763

Monte Sief (2424m) is a subsidiary summit of Col di Lana (2462m), a mountain famous for the key role it played during the First World War (see further 'History' in the Introduction). The peak is a popular snowshoe and ski touring destination as it offers a scenically beautiful ascent on often good snow without any major technical difficulties.

APPROACH

From Arabba, follow the SR48 east towards Pieve di Livinallongo for 5km. Shortly after passing Hotel Al Forte on the right, turn left up a steep winding road to reach the village of Corte. There are parking spaces off the road just short of the village.

Follow the road on foot then at the T junction turn left and head uphill, following signs towards Col di Lana/Sief. At the next set of signposts rejoin the road and continue for 30 metres to a junction, where Sief is signed right and the route to Contrin continues straight on. Follow for Contrin, following sporadic paint markers on the conglomerate rock, which lines the right side of the road.

Monte Sief
(2424m)

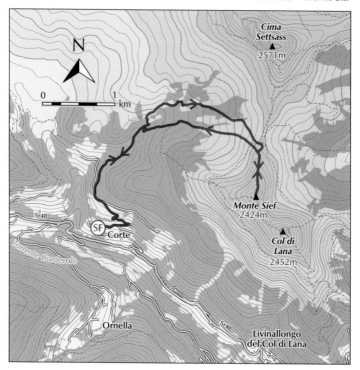

After another 100 metres reach another junction with a snow-covered vehicle track leading to Col di Lana, Sief and Col dla Roda on path 21C. Turn right onto this and follow the track until it opens out into a pretty valley with stunning views of Settsass directly in front. After following the right side of the valley for 25mins, reach a large sign which points right to Col dla Roda, Sief and Col di Lana on path 21C. Ignore this and continue straight on, ascending to reach another track leading off on the right. Ignoring this as well and keeping on the main track, continue to enter into a valley where the path makes a sharp left and begins to traverse the hillside. At an old derelict hut, turn right to almost bear back on yourself and head in the direction of Settsass.

Shortly after the sharp turn right, follow a shallow valley and aim for a newer hut some 80 metres further on, passing this on its left. Continue until the terrain becomes steeper, with two huts on the right. Turn right here, with the peak of

On the summit of Monte Sief

Monte Sief now visible on the right. Pass above the larger of the two huts and turn right, heading due east towards the peak.

From the hut continue for another 80 metres then turn left slightly, heading uphill towards another small hut. There is no set line here so pick the most logical route through the trees, often with lovely powdery snow. Come to the treeline and pass along the top left side of the copse, first following the line of a streambed and then cutting right above the trees to keep above a series of huts to the left, aiming logically for the ridgeline below the summit of Monte Sief.

Continue to ascend for 40mins, staying left along the valley and taking a logical line to reach the prominent saddle, marked with an information board and a sign pointing up to the summit. There are excellent views even from this point, taking in the Tofana and Lagazuoi groups, Averau, Lastoni di Formin, Pelmo and Cristallo. For the full summit experience, continue logically along the ridgeline for 35mins to reach the top of **Monte Sief**.

To descend, return to just before the saddle and drop left into a wide open area, keeping right of the obvious valley below and descending towards an area of small trees by a cluster of huts. In good visibility, use Piz Boè as a point of reference, aiming directly in the direction of this before veering slightly to its right. Pass to the left of the three huts then keep to the right of a shallow canyon, following a blunt ridge to reach two more huts. Pass these on the right, picking a way through the sparse trees.

Where the ridge above the canyon comes to an abrupt end, either drop into the canyon on the left via a steep bank or zigzag through the woods in front, reaching a path on the left and continuing to descend a small valley. A good path leads along a ledge to the left of a streambed to exit onto the main track taken at the start of the route.

From here, retrace the initial part of the route to return to the car.

Other possibilities

This route also makes for an excellent easy ski tour that often offers powder snow due to its north facing aspect (2.1).

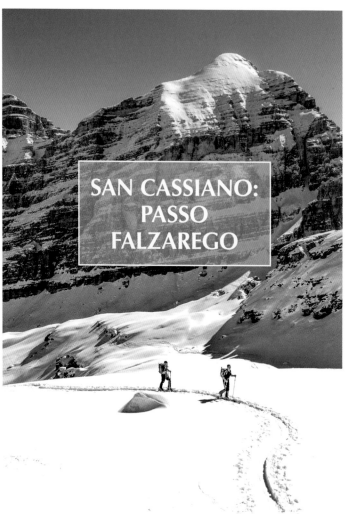

SAN CASSIANO: PASSO FALZAREGO

Ascending perfect snow under the imposing bulk of Tofana di Rozes (3244m)
(Routes 31 and 32)

INTRODUCTION

The Passo Falzarego lies at a crossroads between the Val Badia, Cortina and the Livinallongo valley. It is a scenically stunning location with superb pistes taking in views of the Lagazuoi, Cinque Torri and Tofana di Rozes, as well as panoramas of the Cristallo and Sorapis groups above Cortina. The site of fierce fighting during the First World War, the Falzarego formed part of the frontline between the Italian and the Austro-Hungarian troops who engaged in a long siege of explosive and tunnel warfare in an attempt to dislodge their enemies and gain the higher ground. Although the signs of military activity are less evident in the winter when snow covers much of the remaining trenches and bars access to the tunnels, the marks made by the Great War can still be felt, making this an area which is as poignant as it is beautiful.

Just below the top of the pass stands the iconic formation of Cinque Torri – Five Towers. The towers are a defining symbol of the area and in winter they protrude proudly from the snowy plateau, a breathtaking spectacle of idyllic mountain beauty. The Cinque Torre e Nuvolau snowshoe is perhaps one of the 'must see' snowshoe routes in the area, ascending the airy plateau to Rifugio Nuvolau, the oldest mountain hut in the Dolomites before making a dramatic journey through the spires of the Cinque Torri.

There is also no shortage of superb and varied ski touring possibilities here. Cadin di Fanis takes you on a long but rewarding day through an unspoilt and isolated winter landscape, often with excellent snow, while for more experienced mountaineers the gully descent of Canale della Nonna can be combined with an exciting winter ascent of Via Ferrata Col dei Bos.

Accommodation options on top of the pass itself are limited to rifugios (Rifugio Lagazuoi is particularly well located at the top of the Lagazuoi cablecar, providing the added benefit of first tracks down the freshly groomed slopes either side). However, San Cassiano at the base of the Passo Valparola road more than compensates, with hotels, garnìs, apartments and chalets to suit every budget. The village is also something of a culinary centre, boasting two Michelin-starred restaurants, St Hubertus and La Siriola. For a more affordable option there are numerous restaurants and rifugios in the area, serving a fusion of Italian and Austrian cuisine.

Thanks to good links to the Sella Ronda ski network and excellent road access to the Falzarego, Cortina, Val Badia and San Martino areas, San Cassiano is a great base from which to explore many of the locations described in this guide.

ROUTE 30
Settsass

Start/Finish	Rifugio Valparola (2178m)
Distance	13km
Total ascent	600m
Total descent	600m
Grade	F
Time	5–6hrs
Aspect of ascent	S
Aspect of descent	N
Map	Tabacco No 07
Parking	Rifugio Valparola car park: 46.5317, 11.98871

This technically challenging but highly rewarding snowshoe tours the distinctive formation of Settsass, crossing a variety of terrain and taking in stunning far-reaching views. The route requires a perfectly stable snowpack, especially for the extension to the summit, which also requires some basic mountaineering experience and confidence in moving on alpine terrain. It is also recommended to attempt this route in good visibility, as although there should not be any particular navigational difficulties, due to the nature of the terrain, the consequences of an error may be severe.

APPROACH

The route begins from Rifugio Valparola, located at the top of the Passo Valparola and easily accessible from San Cassiano to the northwest or Cortina to the east. From San Cassiano take the SR37 east for 11km to reach the pass and park in the rifugio car park on the right.

Walk down the left side of the rifugio and take the path leading left, staying above a depression on the left where in the summer the small Lago di Valparola can be seen. After a short distance on level ground reach a summer signpost where the path forks, marking the start of the Settsass circuit. Keep left here, following the

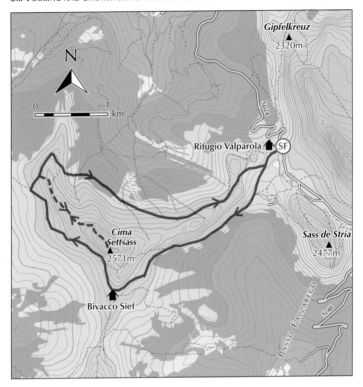

sign for path 23. This path is well-marked but due to the snow cover the waymarks on the rock are often hard to spot and the route is often untracked.

Stay in the line of the summer path, skirting the rock walls along the south side of Settsass, undulating on largely straightforward terrain. Round a smaller formation detached slightly from the main buttresses, Piccolo Settsass, to reach a junction and the wooden hut of **Bivacco Sief**. At this point the route joins with another popular snowshoe ascending from Castello di Andraz (see Other possibilities) and so is often well-tracked. Ignore any tracks leading left across a blunt crest here and keep right, continuing to contour around the mountain following path 23. After hugging closely to the rock walls the path leads out slightly into the more open terrain of the plateau on the left, overlooking the popular Alta Badia piste network.

Continue to reach a junction, where path 23 apparently ends and path 24 is signed left to Rifugio Pralongia and right to Rifugio Valparola. Keep right, following the path which makes a sharp bend right around a cluster of boulders below the summit of Settsass. To reach the summit, turn right here, see Other possibilities.

Continue contouring on challenging terrain characterised by hollows and holes between the rocks of the path. The path skirts the north side of Settsass, staying close to the rock and overlooking a wooded plateau to the left. As the terrain eases, follow the path as it bears left to follow the line of the rocks and returns to the junction with path 23 taken at the start of the route. Turn left here and follow your tracks back to Rifugio Valparola.

THE MOUNTAIN OF SETTSASS

The mountain of Settsass is of particular importance in terms of the history of Dolomites geology. It was here that in 1860 Professor Ferdinand von Richthofen – the uncle, incidentally, of the well-known First World War German fighter pilot Manfred Albrecht Freiherr von Richthofen – first proposed the theory that the Dolomites were in fact derived from coral reefs, adding to the data discovered by Dieudonné Sylvain Guy Tancrede Grater de Dolomieu, Alexander Friedrich von Humboldt and Antonio Catullo, to name just a few of the geologists responsible for charting the complex geological history of this fascinating mountain region.

Sass de Stria (2477m)

Monte Antelao (3264m)

Settsass (2571m)

Settsass from the west

Summit extension

Rifugio Pralongia

Slow progress in deep snow under Settsass

Other possibilities

To reach the summit of **Settsass** (250m above), either ascend direct, weaving through the large boulders and taking care on the very steep terrain to reach the ridgeline (it can be useful to clip the back of the snowshoes down here), or alternatively traverse left delicately along the summer path until the main path continues left and it is possible to make a rising traverse right to join the ridge, then follow this carefully to the cross perched on the panoramic summit. To return, delicately retrace your steps to rejoin the saddle and the main path. Allow an extra hour to take in this extension.

An ascent to Bivacco Sief and the nearby col of Passo Sief from Castello di Andraz on the Falzarego road is a popular route, which has become something of a classic among locals. This ascends from Ristorante La Baita and takes a path leading off from the hairpin just above to reach the ruins of the castle, before ascending through the woods to exit into the open ground by Bivacco Sief. The classic route then turns left to reach the saddle of Passo Sief before descending easily across snowy meadows and woodland to return to the castle.

ROUTE 31
Forcella Grande

Start	Lagazuoi cablecar top station (2752m)
Finish	Armentarola (1650m)
Distance	6km
Total ascent	200m
Total descent	1300m
Grade	F 3.2
Time	3–4hrs
Aspect of ascent	S
Aspect of descent	W/N
Map	Tabacco No 03
Return to start	There are taxi stands at the bottom of the Armentarola ski piste for most of the winter season. If not, a very novel horse tow takes you to Armentarola where an efficient rolling shuttle bus service takes skiers back to the Lagazuoi cablecar.
Parking	Lagazuoi cablecar car park: 46.51948, 12.00826

An excellent route with a short tour leading into two beautiful and rarely frequented couloirs, often containing excellent snow. It is well worth getting up early in order to make the south facing ascent before it gets too hot and to end the route at Rifugio Scotoni in time for lunch, sampling some of the best food in the area.

APPROACH

The route starts from the top station of the Lagazuoi cablecar, situated on top of the Passo Falzarego and easily accessed from San Cassiano to the northwest or Cortina to the east. From San Cassiano take the SR37 east for 12km via the Passo Valparola to arrive just before the junction with the Passo Falzarego, where the large Lagazuoi lift station car park can be found on the left. Take the cablecar to the top.

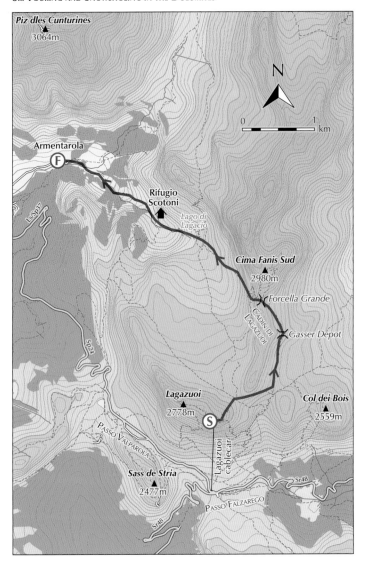

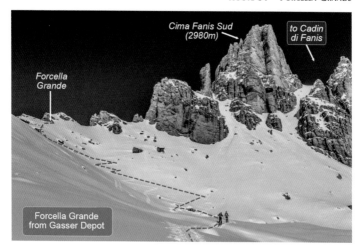

Cima Fanis Sud
(2980m)

to Cadin
di Fanis

Forcella
Grande

Forcella Grande
from Gasser Depot

From the lift station ski down the piste, taking the right-hand fork when the piste splits. Follow the piste until the next bend then exit the piste on the left-hand side. Sidestep or bootpack up the little ridge to the northeast until a change in gradient enables a traverse on skis above or below the avalanche barriers, aiming

Touring underneath Tofana di Rozes

for the saddle of Gasser Depot which can soon be seen splitting the ridgeline to the north. Continue the long traverse, staying as high as possible to reach steeper slopes which lead up to **Gasser Depot** itself. Depending on the conditions, boot-pack or skin up to reach the saddle and make a short ski down the opposite side to enter the **Cadin di Lagazuoi** valley. Ignore any ski tracks descending the valley to the right and instead put skins on and ascend to the northwest, aiming for the ridgeline beneath and to the left of Cima Fanis Sud. Route 32 takes the steep south facing couloir to the right of the peak. Don't forget to look over your shoulder for some spectacular views back towards Tofana di Rozes. Eventually ascend to **Forcella Grande** itself on the left side.

There is a great view down the length of the first couloir from the top, which enables the choice of the best line depending on the snow conditions, usually to be found on the right. Ski down the wide couloir with often excellent snow to reach the wide open slopes below, then keep to the right and aim for the plateau beneath Cima Scotoni. The next couloir is situated to the right of a set of rocky cliffs and to the left of Lago di Lagacio. This is directly above Cima Scotoni and is marked with summer path signposts (path 20). Ski down this to reach **Rifugio Scotoni** and the red ski piste that leads back to Armentarola.

Other possibilities
If the couloir is not in good condition it is possible to turn right onto the Cadin di Fanis itinerary (Route 32) just before the first descent down the initial couloir.

ROUTE 32
Cadin di Fanis

Start	Lagazuoi cablecar top station (2752m)
Finish	Passo Falzarego (1950m)
Distance	10km
Total ascent	800m
Total descent	1600m
Grade	F 2.2
Time	5–6hrs
Aspect of ascent	S
Aspect of descent	N/E/S
Map	Tabacco No 03
Equipment	Crampons, ice axe (a rope can be useful for making the final exposed traverse for less confident parties who are not comfortable with moving on steep terrain)
Return to start	Between late February and late March it is possible to make use of the Dolomitibus service between Borca and the Passo Falzarego to return to the start of the route. The last bus is usually around 4pm but it is worth checking beforehand to ensure the service is running. Alternatively, and if time allows, walk 800 metres up the road to reach the Cinque Torri lift system and use the pistes and three successive lifts (45mins) to return to the Lagazuoi. If time is short and the bus service is not running, either hitch a ride or arrange a taxi for short journey back to the pass.
Parking	Lagazuoi cablecar car park: 46.51948, 12.00826

This long and demanding route allows you to ski the remote and seldom frequented Cadin di Fanis valley, which due to its sheltered and isolated nature often provides excellent snow and the opportunity for fresh tracks a long time after the last snowfall. The route is broken into two distinct sections of ascent and descent; the initial south facing climb up the Cima Fanis Sud couloir is steep and contains a final exposed traverse which should not be underestimated. The return route, which ascends the upper part of the Val

Travenanzes, is scenically stunning but requires good stamina at the end of the day, followed by the final descent of Col dei Bos to return back to the Passo Falzarego.

APPROACH

The route starts from the top station of the Lagazuoi cablecar, situated on top of the Passo Falzarego and easily be accessed from San Cassiano to the northwest or Cortina to the east. From San Cassiano take the SR37 east for 12km via the Passo Valparola to arrive just before the junction with the Passo Falzarego, where the large Lagazuoi lift station car park can be found on the left. Take the cablecar to the top.

From the lift station ski down the piste, taking the right-hand fork when the piste splits. Follow the piste until the next bend then exit the piste on the left-hand side. Sidestep or bootpack up the little ridge to the northeast until a change in gradient enables a traverse on skis above or below the avalanche barriers, aiming for the saddle of Gasser Depot which can soon be seen splitting the ridgeline to

Forcella Grande

Cima Fanis Sud (2980m)

to Cadin di Fanis

Approach to Cadin di Fanis

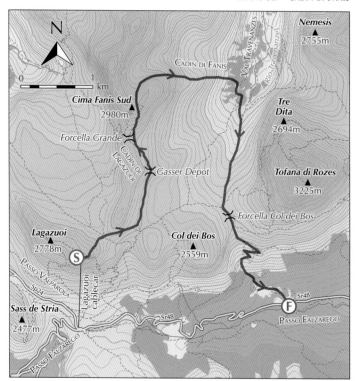

the north. Continue the long traverse, staying as high as possible to reach steeper slopes which lead up to **Gasser Depot** itself. Depending on the conditions, boot-pack or skin up to reach the saddle and make a short ski down the opposite side to enter the **Cadin di Lagazuoi** valley. This provides a good view of Cima Fanis Sud to the northwest, characterised by the large couloir running up the right-hand side that provides the ascent route into the Cadin di Fanis.

Either ascend to the couloir directly or skin up the shallower valley to the left before traversing in rightwards to the base of the couloir proper. Climb the couloir on steep terrain forcing many kick turns or, in icy conditions, necessitating the use of crampons. Reach the top and make a short exposed traverse across a gully (take care as there are cliffs on the right) to reach the start of the beautiful **Cadin di Fanis**.

Ascending the final slope to reach Cadin di Fanis

The valley is wide and provides good opportunities to seek out the best snow conditions during the descent of the steeper initial slope. Reach a flatter area, from where it is possible to stay left to enter into a couloir underneath the rock faces that leads down into the Val Travenanzes or to traverse right before cutting back slightly left, following the natural progression of the valley floor and weaving between rocky cliffs to enter into woodland that leads to the Val Travenanzes. The latter option usually offers better snow but is harder to navigate as it weaves between rocky outcrops.

On reaching the valley floor of the **Val Travenanzes**, put skins back on and turn right to ascend the valley on its left-hand side for around 1hr (it is also possible to go through the trees on the right if conditions are particularly warm) to reach **Forcella Col dei Bos** situated between Tofana di Rozes and Col dei Bos.

Take the skins off again and ski down, following the valley topography and staying to the right of a large boulderfield to enter onto a steeper slope. Descend this, crossing a summer vehicle track (which can be followed to the right through a tunnel for an easier ski) to enter into sparse woodland which leads down to the road of the **Passo Falzarego**.

Other possibilities

If the ascent of the couloir to the right of Cima Fanis Sud is not in good condition it is possible to turn left and join onto the Forcella Grande itinerary (Route 31).

Instead of skinning back up the Val Travenanzes it is possible to turn left and ski all the way down the valley to reach the road north of Cortina (2.1). This is a beautiful but long descent with many flat areas, requiring good navigation as well as crampons and a rope to overcome several exposed sections. The logistics of returning also need to be considered.

ROUTE 33
Canale della Nonna

Start/Finish	Parking on the Passo Falzarego (1850m)
Distance	10km
Total ascent	800m
Total descent	800m
Grade	F 3.2
Time	3–4hrs
Aspect of ascent	S
Aspect of descent	S
Map	Tabacco No 03
Equipment	Ski crampons can be useful if the ascent is icy
Parking	Car park 4km east of the top of the Passo Falzarego: 46.52218, 12.04807

The summit of Col dei Bos (2559m), perched high above the Passo Falzarego, is a popular winter objective which offers superb views over one of the most scenic spots of the Dolomites. Canale della Nonna (the granny's couloir) offers a technical ski that in good conditions provides one of the best ski descents in the area. The south facing aspect of both the ascent and descent requires a careful assessment of the conditions to avoid unstable or icy snow.

APPROACH

From San Cassiano take the SR37 east for 12km via the Passo Valparola to arrive at the junction with the Passo Falzarego just beyond the Lagazuoi cablecar. Turn left here and head downhill towards Cortina on the SR48 for 3km to reach the large Cinque Torri car park clearly signposted on the right. Pass this and continue downhill for another 750 metres to a parking area on the left at the base of a track.

From the car park, follow the pisted track in the direction of Col dei Bos. Where this splits, continue straight on following the smaller of the two tracks (it is also

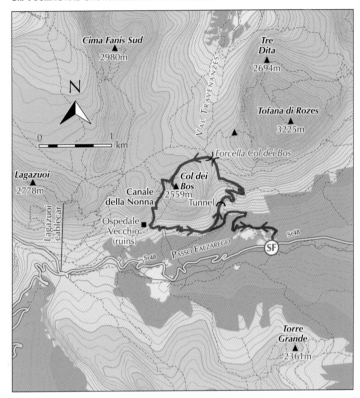

possible continue on the pisted track which joins shortly afterwards) and ascend through the trees for 200 metres to reach a more open area with a large boulder and a hut. Continue through the open meadow, aiming for a bridge and soon rejoining with the main track. Follow the switchbacks of the track to reach and cross the bridge, then continue ascending for 25mins to reach a T-junction.

During this ascent you are surrounded by excellent **views** of the south faces of Tofana and Col dei Bos in front, Cinque Torri, Averau and Nuvolau behind and the Antelao, Cristallo and Sorapis groups over to the right.

Turn right at the junction following for the 402 and 412. Those tempted by a winter ascent of the via ferrata would need to turn left here, see Other possibilities. Ascend the track as it leads through a **tunnel**. Just past the tunnel the terrain opens up and Forcella Col dei Bos becomes visible up high on the left, nestled between Col dei Bos and Tofana di Rozes. Ascend the open slope, overcoming several steep sections forcing kick turns until the gradient eases off, passing above the rock walls to the left until you reach the wide saddle of **Forcella Col dei Bos**. Here turn left, heading south west and following the open slopes to reach the summit cross (and barbed wire) of **Col dei Bos** in a further 30mins.

To descend take the skins off and ski west, aiming just right of the Lagazuoi cablecar (there is sometimes a small cornice to negotiate) until the couloir becomes visible on the left. There are many possible variations and mini gullies within **Canale della Nonna**, many of which require a good snow cover to ski. Fortunately they can be easily observed from above but if in doubt keep right at the first fork and then stay up high, following the summer path to take the subsequent right-hand fork until open slopes lead down to the **Ospedale Vecchio**. These are the ruins of a field hospital from the First World War.

To complete the descent, follow track 423 east, pushing along several flat sections to return to the ascent route and reversing this back to the car.

Tofana di Rozes (3244m)

Col dei Bos (2559m)

Using via ferrata Col dei Bos to access the summit and Canale del Nonna

Other possibilities

For those with suitable mountaineering experience the Col dei Bos/Degli Alpini via ferrata (VF3B), which runs parallel to Canale della Nonna, provides a superb alternative means of ascent (although this should not be underestimated when confronted in winter conditions, requiring suitable equipment and good experience of winter alpine terrain).

For an easier descent or if conditions in the couloir are not ideal it is also possible to ski down your uphill tracks (2.1).

To reduce the amount of height gain it is possible to traverse into the summit from the top of the **Lagazuoi cablecar** using skins to create a more 'freeride' itinerary.

Canale Strobel (3.3), situated to the west of Canale della Nonna, can easily be accessed from the summit of **Col dei Bos** and may provide an interesting alternative to suitably experienced parties.

ROUTE 34
Col dei Bos

Start/Finish	Parking on the Passo Falzarego (1850m)
Distance	10km
Total ascent	800m
Total descent	800m
Grade	F 2.2
Time	5–6hrs
Aspect of ascent	S
Aspect of descent	S
Map	Tabacco No 03
Equipment	Crampons can be useful if the ascent is icy
Parking	Car park 4km east of the top of the Passo Falzarego: 46.52218, 12.04807

This is a popular excursion offering superb views over the Falzarego and Cortina areas under the imposing bulk of Tofana di Rozes (3225m). The south facing aspect of both the ascent and descent requires careful assessment of the conditions to avoid unstable or icy snow.

APPROACH

From San Cassiano take the SR37 east for 12km via the Passo Valparola to arrive at the junction with the Passo Falzarego just beyond the Lagazuoi cablecar. Turn left here and head downhill towards Cortina on the SR48 for 3km to reach the large Cinque Torri car park clearly signposted off on the right. Pass this and continue downhill for another 750 metres to a parking area on the left at the base of a track.

From the car park, follow the pisted track in the direction of Col dei Bos. Where this splits, continue straight on following the smaller of the two tracks and ascend through the trees for 200 metres to reach a more open area with a large boulder and a hut. Continue through the open meadow, aiming for a bridge and soon

Descending from the summit of Col dei Bos and heading back towards Tofana di Rozes

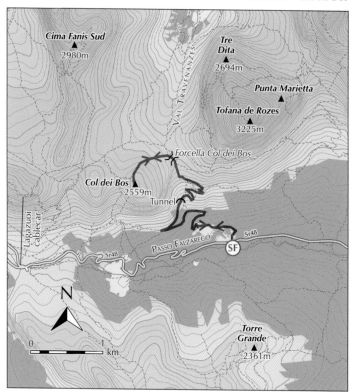

rejoining with the main track. Follow the switchbacks of the track to reach and cross the bridge, then continue ascending for 25mins to reach a T-junction.

Turn right at the junction following for the 402 and 412, ascending the track as it leads through a **tunnel**. Just past the tunnel the terrain opens up and Forcella Col dei Bos becomes visible up high on the left, nestled between Col dei Bos and Tofana di Rozes. Ascend the open slope, overcoming several steep sections forcing kick turns until the gradient eases off, passing above the rock walls to the left until you reach the wide saddle of **Forcella Col dei Bos**. Here turn left, heading south west and following the open slopes to reach the summit cross (and barbed wire) of **Col dei Bos** in a further 30mins.

To descend, reverse the route back to the car.

Taking advantage of a clearing in the trees beneath Cinque Torri

Other possibilities

From the summit of Col dei Bos, the open plateau to the north and the Val Travenanzes both offer additional areas to explore for those wishing to extend the itinerary.

It is possible to create a traverse taking the Lagazuoi cablecar and then descending under the avalanche barriers (stable snowpack required) to descend to Col dei Bos before continuing down along the route described above.

ROUTE 35

Cinque Torri and Nuvolau

Start	Rifugio Scoiattoli (2255m)
Finish	Cinque Torri lift car park (1880m)
Distance	8km
Total ascent	350m
Total descent	725m
Grade	E
Time	3–4hrs
Aspect of ascent	N
Aspect of descent	N
Map	Tabacco No 03
Parking	Rifugio Bai de Dones car park: 46.51903, 12.03786

Situated high above the Passo Falzarego, the five towers of Cinque Torri are one of the most iconic symbols in the Dolomites. As well as offering stunning scenery this snowshoe is steeped in history and allows you to explore some of the trenches and bunkers left by the Italian troops during their standoff with Austria-Hungary in the First World War. This walk has several optional extensions for some additional distance and ascent; otherwise the main route through the Cinque Torri is a good half day excursion. It is predominately downhill and has a couple of narrow, technical sections which require some concentration as you wind your way through the towers.

APPROACH

Cinque Torri can be approached from Cortina in the east or the Alta Badia in the west. From San Cassiano take the SR37 east for 12km via the Passo Valparola to reach the junction with the Passo Falzarego just beyond the Lagazuoi cablecar. Turn left here and head downhill towards Cortina on the SR48 for 3km until arriving at the large Cinque Torri car park, clearly signposted off on the right. Park by Rifugio Bai de Dones at the base of the Cinque Torri chairlift and take the chairlift up to Rifugio Scoiattoli.

From **Rifugio Scoiattoli** you are instantly rewarded with incredible views of Tofana di Rozes, the jagged ridgeline of Croda de Lago and, of course, the towers themselves. The terrace of this quaint rifugio is a great place to have a drink in the sun and take in the surrounding scenery before beginning the walk.

Head south on the service track 439 and begin the ascent towards Forcella Nuvolau, keeping the ski piste to the right to reach **Forcella Nuvolau**.

After taking in the views from the saddle of **Forcella Nuvolau**, which open out to the south revealing the 1000m-high face of Monte Civetta, Monte Pelmo and on a clear day even the highest peak in Austria, the Grossglockner, to the north, you might be satisfied with having a coffee in Rifugio Averau and following your tracks back down.

Continue up along path 439 along the ridge to **Rifugio Nuvolau**.

Rifugio Nuvolau, built in 1883 and purportedly the oldest rifugio in the Dolomites, is closed in winter but the stunning views over the Passo Giau are well worth the ascent, although the ridge can be tricky in heavy snow fall or poor visibility and care should be taken to stay well back from the steep drop and cornice on the right-hand side.

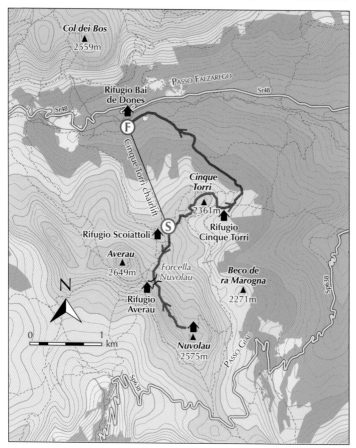

Once at the summit, retrace your steps all the way back down to Rifugio Scoiattoli to begin the descent through the towers of Cinque Torri.

From **Rifugio Scoiattoli** head northeast towards Torre Inglese, the furthest left of the five towers. At a point 50 metres or so before reaching the tower itself, turn right and head towards Torre Quarta (a very square tower with a black face) to become immersed between the imposing towers of rock. In 5mins reach a sign reading Attenzione Sassi (beware of rocks). Turn right here and descend steeply

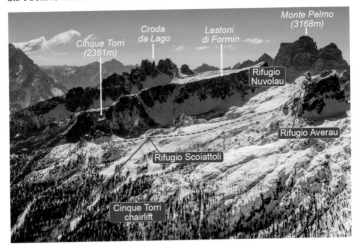

down a narrow gap formed by two towers (Torre Quarta Alta and Torre Quarta Bassa) leaning against each other. Torre Alta is easily distinguishable by the two small trees perched on its top. Walk through this impressive passageway until it opens out, then descend quite steeply on more open terrain. To the northeast the large smooth slab of Torre Trephor, part of the tower which collapsed in 2004, is a useful point of reference to confirm that you're on the right track.

A wooden walkway is usually just visible on the right. Traverse along this and continue in an easterly direction for 15mins to reach a signpost for Rifugio Cinque Torri. Follow the signpost, traversing across the hillside to the south to reach a crest above the riifugio. Continue downhill to reach **Rifugio Cinque Torri** (closed in the winter) and join a service track leading leftwards into the forest. After 10mins reach a sharp hairpin bend as the road bends round to the right. Look out for a small footpath on the left heading into the forest and marked 425 'Bain de Dones', and follow this picturesque path through the trees. Continue down the well marked path following red and white flags and ignoring any turn-offs to return to the car park in 40mins.

Other possibilities

There is the option of beginning the descent through the towers straightaway and not climbing up to Nuvolau (the climb is recommended in good visibility). This option would take 1–2hrs.

ROUTE 36
Tofana di Rozes

Start/Finish	Rifugio Dibona (2080m)
Distance	10km
Total ascent	1200m
Total descent	1200m
Grade	F 3.3
Time	5–6hrs
Aspect of ascent	S/NE
Aspect of descent	NE/S
Map	Tabacco No 03
Equipment	Crampons, ice axe, rope
Parking	Rifugio Dibona car park: 46.52165, 12.08454

The large shield of Tofana di Rozes (3225m) looming above the Passo Falzarego and Cortina is one of the most easily distinguished mountains in the Dolomites and provides an excellent ski mountaineering objective for experienced parties. Although the exposed nature of the peak results in the snow often being in less than perfect condition, this itinerary is very much about the ascent! The route is most commonly tackled in the spring when it is possible to drive up to Rifugio Dibona, thus reducing the amount of ascent. However, it can be enjoyed throughout the winter season with suitably compact and safe snow conditions.

APPROACH

The route is usually approached from Rifugio Dibona located slightly south-east of Tofana di Rozes. Rifugio Dibona can be accessed from Cortina in the east or the Alta Badia in the west. From San Cassiano take the SR37 east for 12km via the Passo Valparola to reach the junction with the Passo Falzarego just beyond the Lagazuoi cablecar. Turn left here, heading downhill towards Cortina on the SR48 for 7km to reach a wooden height barrier on the left marked Parco delle Dolomiti d'Ampezzo and signposted to Rifugio Dibona.

> If the road is passable, drive up to a fork and turn left. The road deteriorates as it ascends to reach a large car park by Rifugio Dibona. Otherwise, park where possible on the Passo Falzarego road and skin up the track to reach the rifugio (1hr, 400m height gain).

From **Rifugio Dibona**, follow a large track west to arrive below the large open slope between Tofana di Rozes and Punta Anna (2731m) and Tofana di Mezzo (3244m). Ascend this easily, cutting back left towards the top and following signs for the summer path. The descent from the Bus de Tofana joins here. Ascend steeper ground now, passing between a series of rocky towers to once again reach a large open area. Turn left here (west), passing the remains of the derelict Rifugio Cantore and keeping right through an area of boulders.

The large northeast slope of Tofana di Rozes is now clearly visible. Make a long rising traverse across this, looking to gain as much height as possible to reach the ridge descending from the summit. Turn left onto the ridgeline and follow

Tofana di Rozes (3225m)

Tofana di Mezzo (3244m)

Punta Anna (2731m)

Bus de Tofana

Alternative approach

Rifugio Dibona

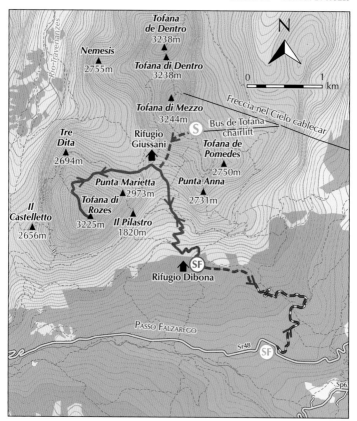

it at an initially easy gradient until it steepens and narrows, forcing the route onto the face on the right. Continue ascending carefully on technically easy but exposed terrain, staying just right of the ridgeline all the way up the large summit cross atop **Tofana di Rozes** to be rewarded with one of the best panoramas in the Dolomites.

To descend, ski down your uphill tracks, taking extreme care on the initial ridge section, which develops above a huge series of cliffs. Turn onto the east face to where the exposure subsides and continue to make a very enjoyable ski descent (although often with challenging snow) down to the valley.

Making the final ascent to the summit of Tofana di Rozes

Other possibilities

It is also possible to approach the initial part of this itinerary from the Bus de Tofana (3.2), a classic Cortina freeride itinerary. This approach usually requires a series of abseils along the Punta Anna via ferrata and some brief sections of climbing, necessitating suitable experience of winter climbing.

From the Cortina ski pistes, take the Freccia nel Cielo cablecar to the large bowl under Tofana di Mezzo and then take the subsequent Bus de Tofana chairlift. From the top of the chairlift ascend the slope behind the chairlift, heading west and aiming for the large buttress (distinguished by pale rock in the lower half and black rock above) above the rock archway (large hole) of the 'bus'. Here, use the wire of via ferrata Punta Anna to descend along the ridgeline (a rope and some abseiling normally required) to reach the large hole of the 'bus'. Pass through this to reach the south side and the descent couloir.

In good conditions it is possible to ski directly from the 'bus'; if conditions aren't ideal it may be necessary to abseil a short way to reach good snow. It is important to wait for the sun to soften the snow to avoid an icy and difficult descent. Ski the couloir, taking care to avoid the exposed rocks, to reach the wide slope on the initial part of the Tofana di Rozes ascent.

SELVA DI CADORE: PASSO GIAU

Skiers on the summit of Monte Mondeval (Route 38)

INTRODUCTION

Nestled between the giants of Monte Pelmo, Civetta, the Marmolada and the Croda da Lago-Cernera Group, the Val Fiorentina is something of an undiscovered gem. Located conveniently between Cortina d'Ampezzo to the northeast and the Zoldo valley leading towards Longarone and Venice to the southeast, the village of Selva di Cadore is a collection of many small hamlets which line the scenic mountain road.

Detached from the more famous ski network of the Sella Ronda, the Val Fiorentina forms part of the Civetta ski area, an excellent option for a day or two on the piste with an assortment of long and varied runs in splendid surroundings. The lift network is best accessed from Pescul, one of the hamlets of the Selva di Cadore region, but can also be joined at Palafavera in the Zoldo area further to the southeast. It is possible to link to the Marmolada and Cinque Torri areas via a ski bus which serves the popular 'Giro della Grande Guerra', a piste circuit which revolves around Col di Lana, one of the bloodiest battlegrounds during the First World War, passing areas of historical interest such as Lagazuoi, Cinque Torri and the Marmolada.

The routes in this guide depart from various locations along the Passo Giau, linking the Val Fiorentina to the Passo Falzarego and Cortina

d'Ampezzo. The justifiably popular Monte Mondeval is an excellent choice for a half day out, with a straightforward ascent culminating in a superbly panoramic peak overlooking Croda da Lago, Becco di Mezzodì, Monte Pelmo, the Marmolada, Civetta, Antelao, Sella, the Tofana groups, the Sesto, Auronzo and Oltrepiave groups, the peaks of Pale di San Martino and Lagorai. Just to the north of Monte Mondeval lies the distinctive ridgeline of Lastoni di Formin, providing a slightly harder tour to the summit plateau before an exhilarating descent through open slopes and tightly packed trees alongside the imposing walls of Croda da Lago. In turn, this ridge formation forms the heart of the Croda da Lago snowshoe, a challenging, steep but scenically stunning route taking in the eponymous lake before encircling the precipitous rock walls of the ridge.

Although the Val Fiorentina is noticeably less developed than the nearby areas of Cortina and Corvara in terms of tourism, there are still plenty of accommodation options to choose from, along with a scattering of pizzerias, restaurants and bars. Selva di Cadore is also the site of the fascinating Vittorino Cazzetta Museum, home to 'L'Uomo di Mondeval', a 7500 year-old skeleton discovered in a Mesolithic burial site on Monte Mondeval.

ROUTE 37
Monte Pore

Start	Rifugio Fedare (2000m)
Finish	Cernadoi (1500m)
Distance	6km
Total ascent	400m
Total descent	900m
Grade	F 3.3
Time	3–4hrs
Aspect of ascent	E
Aspect of descent	N
Map	Tabacco No 03/15
Equipment	Crampons
Return to start	Given the difficult logistics of public transport, this route requires a car drop using two vehicles or a taxi to return to the start point.
Parking	Rifugio Fedare car park: 46.4873, 12.03464

Monte Pore (2405m) is a beautiful and isolated summit characterised by its distinctive pyramidal shape. Located just off the Passo Giau, despite its relatively modest elevation the peak provides commanding views in every direction thanks to its superb location. Descents are possible down any side (see Other possibilities) although the north face (3.3) arguably provides the best and most classic descent in the right conditions. Navigation through the woodland at the end of the route can be difficult and it is worth giving some thought to the logistics of the return.

APPROACH

The route starts from the Rifugio Fedare car park adjacent to the Fedare – Forcella Nuvolau chairlift on the west side of the Passo Giau, 2.5km before the top of the pass. From Selva di Cadore take the SP638 north for 12km following signs for the Passo Giau until reaching the Fedare – Forcella Nuvolau chairlift on the left and parking in the adjacent car park. The logistics of this route need to be considered as the route finishes at the hamlet of Cernadoi on the Passo Falzarego, a 20mins' drive away from Selva di Cadore.

Put skins on and head due west from the car park, following signs for Monte Pore on path 463 and aiming for an evident saddle to the right of the main summit. At the saddle a signpost confirms the way and the ascent can clearly be seen ascending the northeast ridge to the left.

Ascend the ridge direct or on the wider slopes to the right (crampons are sometimes necessary in icy conditions), watching out for the cornice that forms along the left-hand edge after a period of strong wind, to reach the summit cross of **Monte Pore** in 50mins.

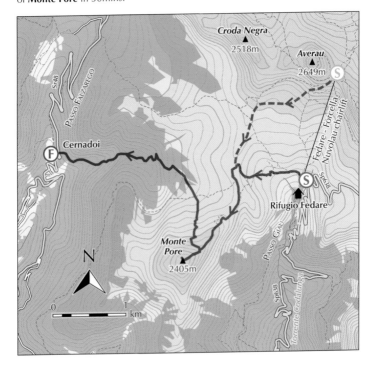

For the descent, most of the faces of Monte Pore can be skied in the right conditions although the north facing slope (3.3) is the most reliable, usually holding the best and most stable snow. Ski down the face that is consistently steep, aiming in the direction of the Lagazuoi and Sass de Stria and following the most obvious line down the valley (take care not to stray too far left).

Continue north and then northwest to reach an open area with a stream on the left; keep right of this and continue towards the left side of a wooden hut at the bottom of a small valley. The skiing here is lovely and gentle on open terrain and is perfect for newcomers to touring who want to practise linking their off-piste turns. The route bears gently left, now aiming for the highest part of Settsass above the Passo Valparola. This section of the route is fairly lacking in features and it is easy to get lost, so keep this as a reference point.

Reach a wooded area where the trees are too dense to ski through easily and descend left into an opening, in turn leading to a larger valley and a more major stream. Keep right of the stream, following the natural terrain and logical gaps through the trees and crossing numerous small streams, trending gently right to reach a narrow forestry track. Cross a bridge over onto the left side of the main stream and follow this to another bridge. This traverses a steep bank and a tributary stream. Continue down to a junction with the path signed to Strada della Vena to the right, marked by a small concrete hut and a stream. Turn right here and continue to another sign; here make a sharp right turn towards Castello

Ascending the final ridge with superb views over the Marmolada

di Andraz, still following the Strada della Vena. When the road of the Passo Falzarego comes into view, drop down to this just above the hamlet of **Cernadoi**.

Other possibilities
For an easier ski, descend the shoulder which was ascended (2.2) on the way up before turning left where the gradient eases to join the north face descent at a series of small wooden huts clustered in an idyllic setting. The south (4.2) and west (3.3) faces both provide skiable descents and are worth researching for experienced parties.

To reduce the amount of ascent it is possible to take the Fedare – Forcella Nuvolau chairlift, ski back down under it and then bear right to join up with the saddle beneath the summit ridge of Monte Pore.

ROUTE 38
Monte Mondeval

Start/Finish	Passo Giau parking (2090m)
Distance	7km
Total ascent	700m
Total descent	700m
Grade	E 2.1
Time	3–4hrs
Aspect of ascent	W/N
Aspect of descent	N/W
Map	Tabacco No 03/015
Parking	Car park 2km east and below the top of the pass: 46.48837, 12.06434

The low technical difficulties of the ascent, the outstanding views from the peak and the north facing wide summit slope that often provides superb powder snow for the descent make this route a true Dolomites classic. The unfortunate consequence of this, however, is that the itinerary can be quite busy, especially at weekends in good weather.

APPROACH

From Selva di Cadore follow SP638 for 11km to the top of the Passo Giau. From here descend for 2km to reach a sharp left hairpin marked by a signpost for path 436 pointing through a gate on the right-hand side. Park in the spaces on the left-hand side.

Put skins on and follow path 436 through the gate. In good visibility the saddle of Forcella Giau is clearly visible to the south. Follow a track on the right side of the valley, staying below the treeline. After 15mins come to a sparsely wooded boulderfield with two prominent boulders directly in front and take a logical line to the right of these. After passing the boulders stay above the treeline to enter into a rocky area; keep right of the rocks and ascend an increasingly steep

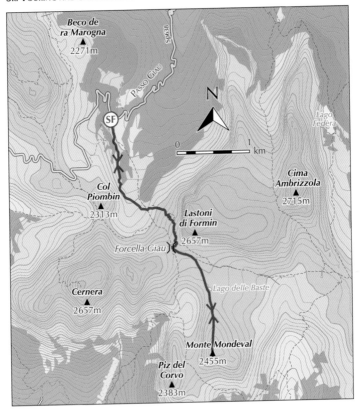

slope up on the right. After a few minutes break into an open valley with superb views of Lastoni di Formin on the left and the col straight ahead. Ascend logically, kick turning as the terrain gets steeper, to soon reach **Forcella Giau**. This rewards with stunning views in all directions, taking in Cinque Torri, Nuvolau, Lastoni di Formin, Pelmo and our destination, Monte Mondeval, to the southeast.

From Forcella Giau the way is clearly visible; ski down in a southerly direction (best to keep your skins on) and enter into the large bowl surrounding **Lago delle Baste**, a beautiful little lake during the summer months. Ascend from here, keeping just left of the easy west ridge, to reach the wide summit plateau and some outstanding views in all directions.

The ski descent to the north is wide and uncomplicated, enabling a number of lines to be selected depending on the number of tracks and the snow conditions coming down from the summit. On reaching flatter ground in the Lago delle Baste basin, put your skins back on to return to Forcella Giau and descend along your uphill tracks back to the car.

215

Descending down the wide initial slope with superb views over the Falzarego and Giau passes

Other possibilities

This itinerary can be combined with Lastoni di Formin (Route 39) to create a long but spectacular traverse of the Passo Giau.

ROUTE 39
Lastoni di Formin

Start	Passo Giau parking (2090m)
Finish	Rifugio Malga Pezie de Paru (1535m)
Distance	10km
Total ascent	650m
Total descent	1200m
Grade	F 2.1
Time	4–5hrs
Aspect of ascent	S/W
Aspect of descent	N
Map	Tabacco No 03
Return to start	This itinerary requires a car drop with a second vehicle or brief taxi ride to return to the start of the route.
Parking	Car park 2km east and below the top of the pass: 46.48837, 12.06434

This is a beautiful traverse of the Passo Giau which unfortunately requires a car drop due to the lack of public transport and the difficulty of hitching with skis up one of the quieter passes in the Dolomites. However, if the logistics can be overcome this ski tour takes in some stunning scenery in a remote environment, culminating in an uncomplicated peak and an often superb ski down.

APPROACH

From Selva di Cadore follow SP638 for 11km up to the top of the Passo Giau. From here descend for 2km to reach a sharp left hairpin, marked by a sign-post for path 436. This points through a gate on the right-hand side where the route starts. For the car drop continue to descend for another 5.5km until a number of signs point left for Rifugio Malga Pezie de Paru; continue for another 50 metres or so to reach the parking area on the right with signpost-ing for the summer path 434 where the route will end.

Put skins on and follow path 436 through the gate. In good visibility the sad-dle of Forcella Giau is clearly visible to the south. Follow a track on the right

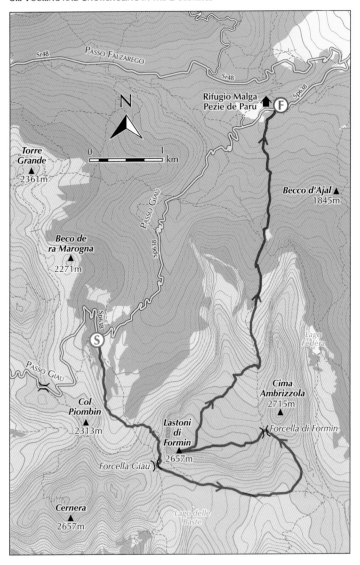

Beginning the ascent towards Lastoni di Formin

side of the valley, staying below the treeline. After 15mins come to a sparsely wooded boulderfield with two prominent boulders directly in front and take a logical line to the right of these. After passing the boulders stay above the treeline to enter into a rocky area; keep right of the rocks and ascend an increasingly steep slope up on the right. After a few minutes break into an open valley with superb views of Lastoni di Formin on the left and the col straight ahead. Ascend logically, kick turning as the terrain gets steeper, to soon reach **Forcella Giau**. This rewards with stunning views in all directions, taking in Cinque Torri, Nuvolau, Lastoni di Formin, Pelmo and Mondeval.

From Forcella Giau, descend slightly to a rocky area on the left, weaving between the rocks below the face of Lastoni di Formin. Keep an eye out for the summer waymarks painted on the ground (some of which are usually visible above the snow) and continue below the face of Lastoni di Formin, descending and then as the ground levels out keeping right of a series of boulders. Reach a wider area with more boulders and keep left.

Rounding the edge of Lastoni di Formin, an obvious valley leads off left to the north, marked by an impressive rock formation at its head (Croda da Lago – Cima Ambrizzola). Ascend the valley, keeping to the right along a blunt shoulder before ascending diagonally left, making a series of kick turns up the final steep section to gain the saddle of **Forcella da Formin**, reached in around 45mins from the bottom of the valley. At the saddle turn left and begin ascending the large sloped plateau to reach the flat summit of **Lastoni di Formin**.

The **views** throughout this journey are superb, taking in Monte Mondeval, Pelmo and Antelao on the route from the initial col and then Lastoni di Formin itself, Croda da Lago, Cortina, the Tofana group and the Cristallo range in the latter half.

From the summit, weave carefully through the dips and hollows of the plateau, heading back towards the walls of Croda da Lago in a northeasterly direction, entering into the valley between Lastoni di Formin and Croda da Lago. The valley is initially gentle and open, making it enjoyable to play up the sides to gain a few steeper turns in what is often excellent snow, before entering the woodland. Here the line is more forced due to the terrain; take a route just right of the stream, crossing back over it here and there and loosely following the summer descent path. Around 200 metres before the end of the rock walls of Lastoni di Formin, keep high and right above the stream, following the summer path. Be sure to avoid getting sucked into the streambed here and instead traverse the hillside until the path forks at Cason de Formin and here turn right onto path 434, signed for Pezie de Paru.

Reach a little hut in an open area and either descend left down a streambed to return to the main track or keep right of the open area, entering into the trees and dropping into another enjoyable gully which also rejoins the main track. Follow the track down to a large metal bridge by a hydraulics plant and a series of signposts. Turn left, crossing the bridge and joining a large forestry track, which you follow to the main road and your vehicle.

Other possibilities
The nearby Mondeval (Route 38) is an excellent option to explore this area with a single vehicle. It is also possible to combine an ascent of Mondeval with this traverse over Lastoni di Formin to create a long but superb mountain day.

ROUTE 40
Croda da Lago

Start/Finish	Ponte de Rocurto (1760m)
Distance	11km
Total ascent	900m
Total descent	900m
Grade	F
Time	5–6hrs
Aspect of ascent	W
Aspect of descent	E/W
Map	Tabacco No 03
Parking	Ponte de Rocurto car park: 46.50537, 12.07751

Set under the dramatic cliffs of Croda da Lago this route allows you to explore the more remote areas around the Val di Formin. With some scrambling and a steep ascent it is a challenging snowshoe, which takes the best part of a day to complete. The altitude and the exposed nature of the walk mean it is best attempted in good visibility, but the incredible views throughout make this a very worthwhile trip.

APPROACH
From Selva di Cadore follow SP638 for 11km to the top of the Passo Giau. From here descend for 5km to reach Ponte de Rocurto (1708m) and park in a long layby on the right-hand side of the road by a signpost marking path 437. The route is also easily accessed from Cortina via the SS48 to Pocol (6km) and then the SP638 towards Passo Giau (4km).

From the layby follow path 437 clearly signed towards Rifugio Croda da Lago/ Palmieri and immediately cross a bridge over the river Costeana just below the road. From here follow the track through the beautiful pine forest which starts off flat but soon begins to climb steeply, revealing the spectacular Tofana di Rozes to the north. Cross another bridge over a small gorge above the river Formin and

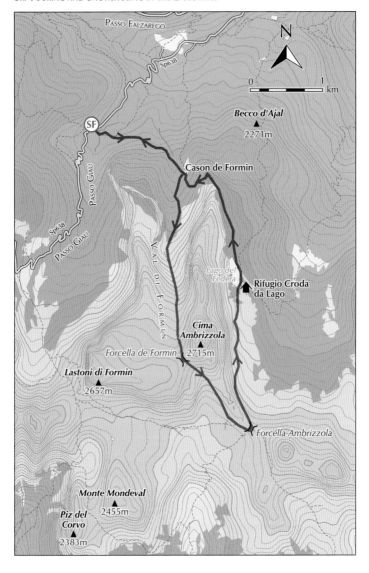

come to a clearing at the **Cason de Formin**. Here the path splits and is signed 434 towards Rifugio Croda da Lago/Palmieri on the left and 435 to Forcella de Formin on the right.

Turn right onto path 435 and continue climbing through the forest until the vegetation recedes and the terrain opens into a narrow valley full of boulders. From here head directly up the valley, zigzagging through the boulders with some scrambling in places. The summer path is marked with the red and white flags but

The stunning Lago del Federa underneath Croda da Lago

some of these will be covered with the snow in the winter so you may need to find your own line through the rocks. Take care to avoid snow hollows.

Continue ascending under the imposing profile of the Croda da Lago towers until the valley opens out to a flatter section leading up to the saddle of Forcella de Formin. If the path becomes hard to follow, try to keep to the left of a small stream and head in a southeasterly direction to **Forcella de Formin**. Here the views open out onto the rolling meadows of Mondeval and the magnificent north face of Monte Pelmo.

Begin the descent, which winds its way quite steeply down to the flat open fields below. Traverse under the cliffs of Cima Ambrizzola and continue straight on along path 436 which begins to climb up to **Forcella Ambrizola**, nestled between the Croda da Lago and Beco de Mezodi. This provides the first glimpse down onto the Lago del Federa and the spectacular ring of mountains which surround the town of Cortina. A signpost points to Rifugio Croda da Lago/Palmieri on path 434; this path is part of the Alta Via delle Dolomiti and is a much more substantial track. Descend this to **Lago del Federa** and **Rifugio Croda da Lago** (only open at weekends with advanced booking in winter), and follow the path behind the hut and back in to the forest. Continue on flat ground through the trees, occasionally getting glimpses down into Cortina below and across to Cinque Torri in the west. After 20mins the path descends steeply to rejoin the junction at **Cason de Formin**. Retrace your steps down path 437 to return to the layby.

PECOL:
VAL DI ZOLDO

Enjoying fresh tracks under the watchful gaze of Monte Pelmo
(Route 42)

INTRODUCTION

The Val di Zoldo is the logical continuation of the Val Fiorentina to the north, accessed via the scenic and surprisingly quiet Passo Staulanza. Much like its neighbouring valley, Zoldo is dotted with numerous small and traditional villages, the key ones being Pecol, Mareson, Pianaz, Coi, Brusadaz, Costa and Fusine. The name of the latter, meaning forge, harks back to the area's ancient industrial tradition of mining and mineral smelting (Fusine is in fact still home to the ruins of an ancient forge) but Zoldo is now better known for its excellent production of artisan ice cream. In fact, European Artisan Gelato Day (yes, it's a real thing!) held in late March was born in nearby Longarone and celebrates local traditionally made Italian ice cream.

Palafavera and Pecol give excellent access to the Civetta ski area, which provides some excellent long tree runs, superb views and bus links to the Marmolada, Sella Ronda and Cortina ski areas for those who wish to travel further afield.

The less-developed nature of this hidden gem of the Dolomites means that, although skiing options are slightly more limited than elsewhere, the snowshoeing possibilities are superb and it is not uncommon to see local families laden with backpacks and snowshoes heading off into the trees. There are three snowshoe routes in this guide: Città di Fiume, Lago di Coldai and Spiz de Zuel. Città di Fiume is in fact the name of a rifugio – sadly closed in the winter – but which makes for an excellent destination for a well-deserved picnic after traversing under the steep and imposing walls of Monte Pelmo.

Spiz de Zuel, beginning from the hamlet of Chiesa on the road towards the Passo Duran, is another popular option suitable for ski tourers and snowshoers alike. The route follows old, snow-covered military roads above Chiesa and crosses through idyllic winter pastures to reach the scenic rounded summit, the final ascent rewarding with views of the Civetta-Moiazza, Antelao-Sorapis and Tofana groups and the more distant peaks of the Belluno Prealps and Friulian Dolomites.

Although quieter than other areas of the Dolomites, much like the neighbouring Val Fiorentina, the Val di Zoldo has a good selection of hotels, garnìs and apartments, and with four star hotels to basic apartments, there is generally something for most budgets. Hardier travellers can make use of the campsite, too, which opens in winter and is located right next to the ski lifts in Pecol. There are a number of restaurants and pizzerias dotted around the various hamlets of the valley to suit most tastes and a couple of small shops for self-catering supplies.

ROUTE 41
Col de la Puina

Start/Finish	Parking 1km north of the top of the Passo Staulanza (1663m)
Distance	6km
Total ascent	650m
Total descent	650m
Grade	F 2.1
Time	3–4hrs
Aspect of ascent	SW
Aspect of descent	SW
Map	Tabacco No 015
Parking	Car park adjacent to the Rifugio Città di Fiume turning: 46.418675, 12.094540

This is a straightforward but beautiful itinerary to the summit ridge of Col de la Puina (2254m) at the base of Monte Pelmo. Although it takes in 600m of ascent the gradient is gentle and continuous and the descent wide and open, making it a lovely half day tour in the quiet Pelmo group.

APPROACH

From Pecol drive north on the SP251 following signs for the Passo Staulanza. Reach the top of the pass with Rifugio Staulanza on the left and continue down five hairpin bends to a car park set just back from the road on the left. There is a sign here for Rifugio Città di Fiume, which usually opens from mid February onwards.

At the back of the car park, next to the sign for Rifugio Città di Fiume, pick up the start of the service track marked 467. Follow this as it climbs gently up through the forest for 20mins to pass the small farm of Malga Fiorentina on the left. Turn right at the junction here and continue on the service track towards Rifugio Città di Fiume, marked on the signpost. After a further 15mins the trees start to thin and

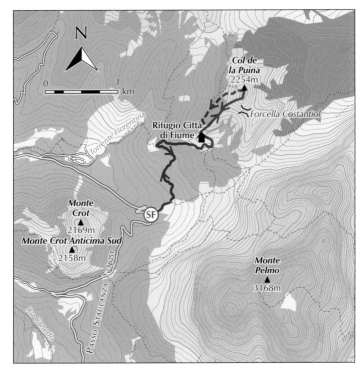

the terrain broadens out into the open area of the valley where **Rifugio Città di Fiume** is located.

To the right a signposted junction marks the point where paths 467, 472 and 480 cross each other. Leave the service track here and move up and left behind the rifugio, away from any of the marked paths. Continue up the obvious ridge covered in trees and take a central line on the ridge itself, winding through the sparse trees in a northeasterly direction. As you ascend the trees recede, allowing you to appreciate the great bulk of Monte Pelmo (3168m) filling the skyline to the south and the dark jagged ridgelines of Croda de Lago and Lastoni di Formin over to the north. Once you reach the summit ridgeline turn left where the gradient increases considerably, often forcing you to take your skis off and boot-pack the final 100m of ascent to the summit. This final steep ascent is rewarded with incredible views over Antelao, 'The King of the Dolomites', and the majestic

Descending Col de la Puina in deep powder

massif of Monte Cristallo set high above the town of Cortina. Continue north along the flat ridge to reach the summit cross of **Col de la Puina** at 2254m.

From the summit retrace your steps following the best snow. Descend back along the rifugio service track to the car park, taking care to avoid snowshoe walkers and cross country skiers who may be ascending.

Other possibilities
With a good covering of snow it is possible to ski back down the steeper west face (2.3 – this requires a stable snowpack) and traverse back left at the bottom of the main face to rejoin the ascent just above the rifugio.

ROUTE 42
Città di Fiume

Start	Top of the Passo Staulanza (1766m)
Finish	Parking 1km north of the top of the Passo Staulanza (1663m)
Distance	10km
Total ascent	250m
Total descent	350m
Grade	E
Time	4–5hrs
Aspect of ascent	W
Aspect of descent	W
Map	Tabacco No 015
Return to start	From here, either hitch back to the top of the pass (the area is popular with snowshoe walkers and so it is often possible), await one of the sporadic buses which serve the Passo Staulanza in high season or walk back along the side of the road to return in around 30mins.
Parking	Passo Staulanza car park: 46.4207, 12.1042

This is a popular and consequently often well tracked route to the pretty Rifugio Città di Fiume below Monte Pelmo. The short length and easy descent make it an ideal half day excursion but arranging return transport back to the pass is advised to avoid the 30mins' walk uphill back to the car.

APPROACH

From Pecol drive north on the SP251 for 6.5km, following signs for the Passo Staulanza. Park on the left at the top of the pass just before Rifugio Staulanza.

From the rifugio walk northeast down the road towards Selva di Cadore, passing a path on the right signed to Rifugio Venezia on path 472. Ignore this and continue to where the road bends to the left, approximately 80 metres from the car park, where Rifugio Città di Fiume can be seen through the trees. A sign standing 20 metres off the path points uphill – at this point come off the road onto the path and follow a sign to Rifugio Città di Fiume, leading through the woods then

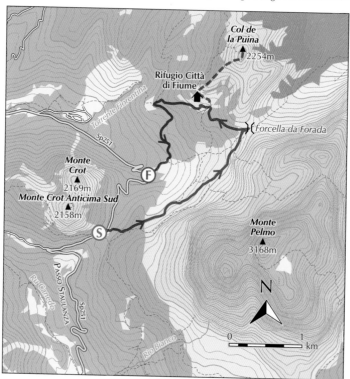

turning right to ascend steeply. The path markers are faded and quite sparse on this section; as such the route may be difficult to navigate without tracks, so be careful to note each waymark and be prepared to backtrack if they become lost from sight. Ten minutes after leaving the road the path merges with a variation of path 472 joining from the Passo Staulanza.

Here path 480 is signed straight on; ignore this and stay on path 472, aiming for the rifugio which can be glimpsed through the trees. Keep following the markers, weaving through the trees on fairly level ground and with more frequent waymarks than in the previous section. Continue for 10mins to exit the trees, where the ascent to this point is rewarded by a broad and scenic view taking in Monte Pelmo on the right, Col de la Puina directly ahead and Rifugio Città di Fiume down to the left below the hill. There are also tantalising glimpses of the distinctive Lastoni di Formin and Croda da Lago ridgelines above Cortina.

Now on much more open terrain, begin traversing the slope, keeping high on the right and taking a line some 200 metres below the rocks of Monte Pelmo. Aiming for an obvious col directly in front, pass a large boulder after 300 metres followed by a second boulder 200 metres further on, both providing good landmarks in poor visibility. Continue in the same line, taking care on the traverse as the angle of the slope can make movement difficult, particularly with a soft layer of snow over harder packed snow or ice, to reach **Forcella da Forada** in around an

Traversing underneath Monte Pelmo

hour from exiting the trees. Your efforts are rewarded with a view down the other side of the col to the pretty Val de Forada.

From the col turn left and follow the well-signed path 480 moving downhill through the trees to reach **Rifugio Città di Fiume** in 15mins. It is open on certain dates in the winter but is surrounded by picnic benches and offers fantastic views even when closed, making it an ideal lunch spot.

After a well-earned break at the rifugio begin descending the large pisted track, looking out for the tobogganists who often make use of this at the weekends. After 10mins continue past an Agriturismo, a small country farm building, on the right and continue down the track for a further 20mins to reach the Passo Staulanza road at hairpin no 3.

Other possibilities

The summit of Col de la Puina provides a worthwhile objective for confident parties (around 1hr 30mins there and back). Follow the obvious ridgeline up behind Rifugio Città di Fiume taking care as the ridge narrows towards the top.

ROUTE 43
Rifugio Venezia traverse

Start/Finish	Rifugio Palafavera (1520m)
Distance	12km
Total ascent	450m
Total descent	450m
Grade	E
Time	5–6hrs
Aspect of ascent	S/E
Aspect of descent	E/S
Map	Tabacco No 015
Parking	Rifugio Palafavera car park: 46.4021, 12.10115

This steep woodland ascent leads to a dramatic traverse directly under the imposing south and east faces of Monte Pelmo (3168m), offering spectacular views over to Monte Civetta (3220m), Antelao (3264m) and Cima dei Preti (2703m). The final uphill approach through the trees before the long traverse can be difficult to navigate and requires a good sense of direction.

APPROACH

From Pecol follow the SP251 north for 2km and park at Rifugio Palafavera on the left, opposite the Palafavera campsite.

Turn left out of the car park and walk up the road for 200 metres, passing the **Palafavera campsite** to reach a signpost on the right-hand side. Turn right here, following for the 474. The path skirts around the top of the campsite before joining up with the path coming out of the campsite by a signpost. It is possible to join path 474 from the southeast corner of the campsite but the owners would prefer people not to walk through the site. Make a sharp turn to the left following signs for Trans Pelmo and Rifugio Venezia. Pass another signpost confirming the way then after 20mins reach a junction with path 498.

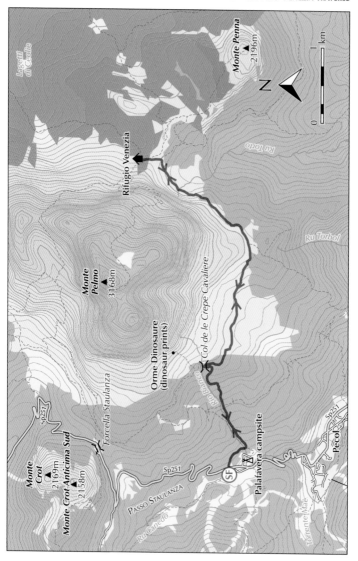

The signposting is a little confusing here but follow the sign indicating 'Orme Dinosaure' ('Dinosaur Footprints') which points straight on. The path begins to ascend more steeply through the trees and the way markers become more sporadic, largely due to the fact that many of them are marked on the rocks and as such are covered with snow in the winter.

If you lose sight of the markers completely, the route essentially heads east with a small deviation left around an area of small cliffs, aiming directly for the lower slopes of Monte Pelmo which can be glimpsed through the trees (if in doubt keep slightly left). As the path gains height the trees give way to dwarf pines. Continue for 30mins to reach **Col de le Crepe Cavaliere** (1900m) signpost where path 472 intersects. Turn right onto path 472, signposted for Rifugio Venezia, and traverse with easy navigation and stunning views for 1hr 30mins to reach a crossroads with paths 475 and 471. Turn left to reach the superbly situated **Rifugio Venezia** in a further 15mins of beautiful walking.

To return, retrace your steps back to the car.

Other possibilities

The route is often started from the top of the Passo Staulanza at **Forcella Staulanza** following path 472. This reduces the amount of ascent but does make for a slightly longer route.

ROUTE 44
Spiz de Zuel

Start/Finish	Chiesa outskirts (1390m)
Distance	12km
Total ascent	800m
Total descent	800m
Grade	E
Time	5–6hrs
Aspect of ascent	S
Aspect of descent	S
Map	Tabacco No 015
Parking	Outskirts of Chiesa: 46.34453, 12.10236

The rounded peak of Spiz de Zuel (2033m) is one of the classic winter destinations of the Val di Zoldo. The route is straightforward and as the ascent takes place largely in the trees, this is a good option for warm spring days when the shade provides welcome respite from the sun. The relentless ascent develops on easy terrain and the stunning views from the summit more than compensate for the effort.

APPROACH

From Pecol follow the SP251 south for 6km to reach the hamlet of Dont. Turn right into the village onto the SP347, following signs for the Passo Duran. This is a very narrow road with passing places, so take care on blind bends. Continue for 3km to pass the turn-off to the village of Chiesa and continue for another 1km to reach the junction leading right to Val della Grava. Park in the parking area just by the junction.

From the parking area, join onto the narrow tarmac road signed towards Rifugio Coldai and Rifugio Torrani, following summer path waymarks for path 557. This ascends at a moderate gradient, passing a number of wooden huts, and instantly rewards with striking views towards Moiazza and Monte Civetta. The road is

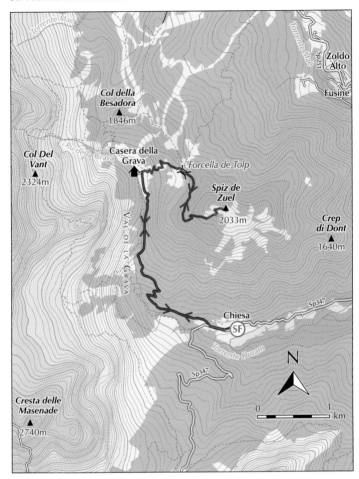

usually cleared and pisted in the lower section, although after heavy snowfall snowshoes are often required as soon as you leave the car park. The track soon enters the woodland and begins to ascend more steeply, switchbacking relentlessly before reaching a flatter section which provides a little respite. Ignoring paths branching off to Triol dei Brusadai and Bivacco Grisetti, continue along the

Ascending through beautiful woodland

road to where the landscape opens out dramatically, soon reaching the snow-covered farm buildings **Casera della Grava**.

Just to the right of the farm, turn right to join onto path 584, an old military road which leads east and can be easily distinguished even when untracked. Continue at a consistent gradient, taking in views of Monte Pelmo to the north east and Civetta to the west. Just below Forcella del Tolp, continue logically along the track as this bears south to reach a shoulder below the summit. Forcella del Tolp is accessible via a short detour and provides an excellent view over the mountains to the north.

Ascend more steeply up the final summit slopes to reach the top of **Spiz de Zuel**, in fact formed of two elevations of almost identical height (2035m and 2033m). The view from the summit is truly breathtaking, encompassing the mountains of Pelmo, Bosconero, Spiz di Mezzodì, Antelao and the nearby mountains of Moiazza and Civetta to name but a few.

After a well-deserved pause, reverse the route to return to the car in **Chiesa**.

CORTINA AND MISURINA: PASSO TRE CROCI AND TRE CIME

*Leaving Rifugio Auronzo and beginning
the traverse towards Forcella Lavaredo (Route 49)*

INTRODUCTION

Although Cortina's reputation for glitz, glam and celebrity fame precedes it, the town offers a great base for the more frugal sports of ski touring and snowshoeing. Located in the Ampezzo basin and surrounded by some of the most striking peaks in the Dolomites, it earns its picture-postcard reputation and, unlike much of the area, reserves a purely Italian feel.

Col Rosa, a modest yet distinctive peak located to the northwest of the town, offers an excellent circular snowshoe taking in a variety of views and even a glimpse of the frozen Cascate di Fanes waterfalls.

Northeast of Cortina lies Lake Misurina. The largest lake in the Cadore region, it was the venue for the Winter Olympic speed skating races in 1956. The lake is also the subject of local folklore. One tale tells of how Misurina begged her uncle, King Sorapis, to buy her a magic mirror from a local witch. The witch agreed to sell the mirror, but demanded that in return she could turn the King into stone to shade her garden. The king agreed, and the witch turned him into the huge mountain known today as Sorapis. On learning of her uncle's sacrifice, Misurina cried and cried, her tears pooling to form the lake at the foot of her uncle's mountain.

On a more prosaic note, Misurina is also the gateway to the Dolomites' most iconic feature – the Tre Cime di Lavaredo. The cluster of monoliths is arguably one of the most memorable views in the world and in summer the paths which encircle it are overrun with walkers, climbers and tourists. In the winter, it is not uncommon to have the Giro delle Tre Cime entirely to yourself, a truly magical winter experience.

The imposing bulk of the Cristallo massif lies equidistant between Cortina and Misurina, a complex labyrinth of rock walls, towers and couloirs. A ski touring ascent up to Passo Cristallo with a subsequent descent of the beautiful Val Fonda provides the classic itinerary for parties of suitable experience.

Thanks to Cortina's reputation, accommodation tends to be more expensive than in other areas, but in addition to the luxury hotels there are more affordable B&Bs, apartments and campsites. Misurina, although small, is well served for accommodation and even has a convenience store for lunches and self catering supplies. Continuing north from Misurina, beyond the lesser known Lago di Landro, is the town of Dobbiaco. Decidedly more Austrian in feel, with the Austrian border just 13km to the west, Dobbiaco has a diverse range of accommodation options but is less well placed than Cortina and Misurina for accessing the ski lifts and other areas described in this book.

ROUTE 45
Malga Ra Stua

Start/Finish	Sant' Uberto (1400m)
Distance	10km
Total ascent	350m
Total descent	350m
Grade	E
Time	3–4hrs
Aspect of ascent	S
Aspect of descent	S
Map	Tabacco No 03
Parking	Sant' Uberto car park: 46.60306, 12.1061

This easy and popular snowshoe up to the family-run Malga Ra Stua Rifugio has many different optional extensions. This area was witness to the first casualties in the Dolomites when Italy declared war on Austria-Hungary and made an assault on Croda de R'Ancona, marking the start of the Ampezzo basin conflict during the First World War. To bring supplies and reserve troops to this area, the Austrian army constructed a road between Ra Stua, Lerosa and Cimabanche. This road provides the optional 'Forcella Lerosa' extension and is highly recommended (if the logistics of returning can be overcome) both for its historical significance and for the stunning views of the dramatic Croda Rossa (3146m).

APPROACH

From Cortina take the SS51 north following signs to Dobbiaco for 8km until the road makes a large hairpin turn to the right. Turn left here into the large Sant' Uberto car park.

From the top of the car park follow the pisted track north on path 6, following signposting towards Malga Ra Stua. Ignore the smaller path 6, which branches off to the left (this forms the descent route) and right (a higher traverse which

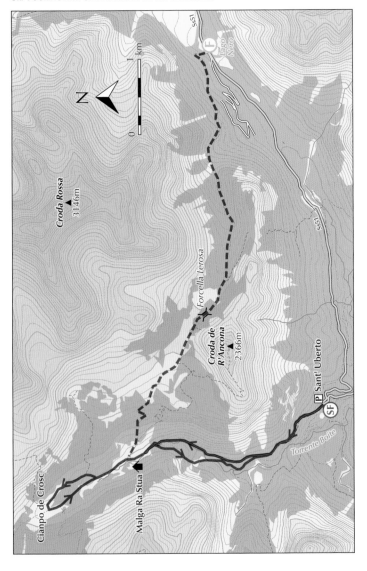

is not recommended in the winter), and continue following the large track to shortly reach a clearing with spectacular views to the west. Continue following the large track for another 3km with easy navigation to reach **Malga Ra Stua**. This is a superb spot for refreshments.

Continue north past the rifugio, ignoring path 8 which turns off right. This is the turn to take for the Forcella Lerosa extension, see Other possibilities. There are many possible lines now, choosing between the left side of the valley, the valley floor (large track 6) or the smaller path (also marked 6) that traverses the right side of the valley to reach **Campo Croce**.

Campo Croce translates as 'cross field' and was the burial site of some of the first casualties in this area during the First World War. Although you can turn around whenever you wish, it is worth continuing as far as the entrance to the Salata Valley which cuts between the impressive rock walls to the north and provides an excellent vantage point from which to view the surrounding scenery.

To return, continue the loop to retrace your steps back to Malga Ra Stua. Just past the outbuildings turn right, crossing a bridge over the river and following a well marked path that descends through the woods and runs parallel to the large track ascended on the walk in. After 1km reach a junction and turn left to rejoin the track. Follow this for a further kilometre to reach the car park at **Sant' Uberto** again.

The vantage point that made this area so contested during the First World War

Other possibilities

Forcella Lerosa provides a superb and highly recommended extension if you have two vehicles or are happy to consider hitching or getting a taxi. Just north of **Malga Ra Stua** turn right onto path 8, heading east and following for Forcella Lerosa. Shortly afterwards ignore a smaller path leading off right; this is a summer shortcut and is not recommended in the winter. Follow the track which leads steeply uphill through dense forest to reach a large clearing between the hugely impressive rock walls of Croda Rossa (3146m) to the north and Croda de R'Ancona (2366m) to the south.

Continue uphill for another kilometre to reach **Forcella Lerosa** (2020m) itself, now with fantastic views to the east as well. Descend the opposite side towards Cimabanche dropping into the beautiful Val Gotres, which shortly yields a spectacular view of the iconic Tre Cime di Lavaredo. Continue following the track as this descends back into trees, eventually leading logically to the road (SS51), 1km short of the hamlet of Cimabanche.

ROUTE 46
Posporcora and Col Rosa circuit

Start/Finish	International Camping Olympia (1340m)
Distance	14km
Total ascent	400m
Total descent	400m
Grade	E
Time	5–6hrs
Aspect of ascent	E
Aspect of descent	E
Map	Tabacco No 03
Parking	Car park adjacent to International Camping Olympia: 46.56867, 12.11592

This long and demanding snowshoe encircles the perfectly formed remote peak of Col Rosa (2166m) and is a classic of the Cortina area. While the route predominantly unfolds through woodland there are many excellent and ever changing viewpoints over the Ampezzo basin and the Fiames and Fanis groups.

APPROACH

The route starts from just outside the Camping Olympia complex situated to the north of Cortina. From Cortina take the SS51 north, following signposts to Dobbiaco for 5km until reaching the well signposted turn off for International Camping Olympia. Turn left here and drive over the bridge, parking on the opposite side and taking care to avoid the private parking spaces belonging to the campsite.

From the parking area follow signs south for path 409 signposted towards Lago Ghedina along a large track. After 15mins reach **Parueto** (1445m) and turn right following for path 409 towards Passo Posporcora.

Continue for another 15mins as the path begins to ascend more steeply, ignoring a left turn for path 410 to reach **Sote I Crepe** (1649m) and another junction with path 410. Turn right, still following path 409 for Posporcora, and follow the switchbacks of the track as it ascends west and then north for 30mins. Finally the gradient eases and the path begins to traverse, providing spectacular views overlooking the Ampezzo basin.

Follow the path as it bends sharply to the left, ignoring an unsignposted path and continuing straight on to reach **Jou dei Comate** (1777m) and a junction with

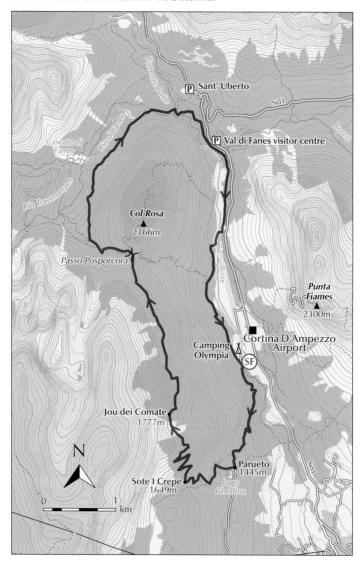

path 446 which turns off to the left. Ignore this and carry straight on along path 409, traversing with great views for 40mins to reach **Passo Posporcora** (1720m).

Now turn left (west) onto path 408, descending steeply through some beautiful woodland and enjoying some tantalising glimpses towards the Fanis group. After 20mins reach another junction and turn right, leaving path 408 and continuing to descend for another 35mins to reach a large track that intersects horizontally. Turn right onto this (path 10-401) and follow it for 25mins, ignoring numerous turn offs, to reach the **Val di Fanes visitor centre** car park. Aim for a track which branches off from the bottom right corner of the car park signposted for Cortina. This leads down to the river, which is followed on its left side to reach a wooden bridge. Cross the bridge onto the right side of the river and follow the path through woodland to turn left onto a large track (path 417). Follow this all the way back, passing the **campsite** and reaching the parking area in 25mins.

Other possibilities
Bearing in mind that this is already a long day, the route can be extended to the Cascate di Fanes icefall, which is spectacular in the winter. However as a full appreciation of the fall involves a traverse of an exposed ledge along a brief section of via ferrata wire, this can be a serious proposition in the winter and should not be underestimated.

Enjoying excellent views of the Ampezzo region making the beautiful traverse to Posporcora

To view the icefall, descend from **Passo Posporcora** then at the first junction ignore the turn-off right described above and continue straight on along path 408. Reach a crossroads and take the well signed path 401 right to reach a picnic area. Continue following signs to reach the exposed traverse, from where via ferrata wire leads along a ledge to provide a view of **Cascate di Fanes** icefall. To return, follow path 10-401 back downhill to the **Val di Fanes visitor centre** car park and continue as above.

ROUTE 47
Forcella Faloria traverse

Start	Rio Gere (1700m)
Finish	Acquabona (1120m)
Distance	9km
Total ascent	620m
Total descent	1200m
Grade	F 2.2
Time	4–5hrs
Aspect of ascent	N
Aspect of descent	S
Map	Tabacco No 03
Return to start	From Acquabona the frequent Linea Urbana No 2/2a/2b bus service leads back to Cortina bus station adjacent to the Faloria cablecar. The bus runs more or less hourly between early January and early April. Take the cablecar and follow the ski pistes back to the parking area at Rio Gere.
Parking	Rio Gere car park: 46.55116, 12.18996

Although this route is often done as a freeride descent using the Faloria lift systems out of Cortina, a traverse from the top of the Passo Tre Croci makes for a more complete and varied itinerary. Return to your vehicle is possible via a bus back to Cortina and then a descent down the pistes from the top of the Faloria cablecar back to the car park at Rio Gere. This route requires good snow cover for a satisfying descent and is usually best tackled in the spring.

APPROACH

From Cortina take the SR48 east following for the Passo Tre Croci for 6km to reach the large parking area of Rio Gere, opposite the rifugio of the same name.

From the highest point of the **Rio Gere** car park in the northeast corner, follow path 209 which runs parallel to the road to reach the top of the **Passo Tre Croci**. Branch off the road onto a forestry track behind the hotel at the pass, often pisted in the winter as a cross-country ski route. Follow this for 500 metres to where the piste bears right; exit left onto path 213, ascending through the trees to reach an open clearing. At the fork in the clearing, turn right and ascend a series of small valleys, aiming for a small hill topped with a lone pine tree. Cross this and undulate down and back up before skirting the rocks towards a series of terraces below a prominent face. Continue straight on beyond these to reach the saddle of **Forcella Faloria**. From here the Val Orita is clearly visible below.

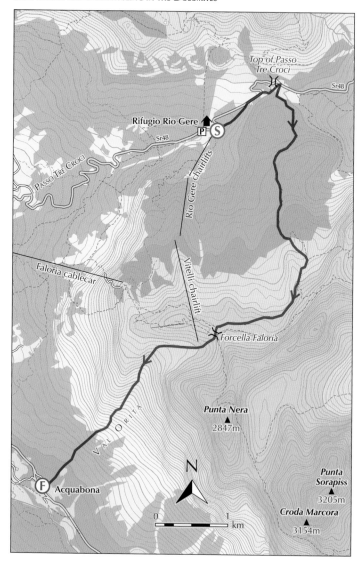

Descending the Val Orita

Ski down the initial slope, which sometimes has a small cornice at the top, traversing to the right just above the valley floor and aiming for a craggy outcrop further to the right. This drops into a steeper area where the descent continues between rock walls, aiming for an area of sparse trees at the bottom. Here either weave between sparse vegetation along the valley floor or traverse high on the left before turning right onto a large open slope (steeper option). Ski down the open slope, keeping to the right until entering the trees 100 metres above the main forest with a rightwards traverse. This section is difficult to navigate if there are no tracks but essentially the route descends to the right, following sparse markers on the trees and forestry tracks to arrive at the small hamlet of **Acquabona**.

Other possibilities

If the conditions in the Val Orita aren't suitable or if the valley is tracked out, it is possible to ski down your uphill tracks, albeit encountering several flat sections (2.1).

To ski the Val Orita without the uphill tour take the **Vitelli chairlift**, easily accessed using the Faloria cablecar or the chairlifts from Rio Gere. From the top of the lift turn left and ski along the top of the ridge until it is possible to drop into the **Val Orita** to the right (many possible entrances).

ROUTE 48

Passo del Cristallo

Start	Top of the Passo Tre Croci (1810m)
Finish	Rio Val Fonda parking (1440m)
Distance	9km
Total ascent	1000m
Total descent	1370m
Grade	PD 2.2
Time	5–6hrs
Aspect of ascent	S
Aspect of descent	N
Map	Tabacco No 03
Equipment	Crampons, ice axe
Return to start	Given the difficult logistics of the return, a second vehicle or a taxi ride is recommended for this route. Alternatively it is possible to convert the route as an out-and-back itinerary (see Other possibilities), negating the need for a return journey.
Parking	Passo Tre Croci: 46.5568, 12.20172

This is a classic itinerary that carves its way through the heart of the Cristallo group, crossing some striking and impressive terrain and culminating in a long and beautiful north facing descent towards Dobbiaco. The route should not be underestimated as the ascent is long, steep and doesn't follow any summer path markers, requiring an experienced and fit party. Due to the south facing aspect of the ascent it's worth making an alpine start during periods of warm weather. To complete the full traverse you need to have a second vehicle or organise a taxi for the return journey.

APPROACH

If you intend to use a taxi for the return journey, from Cortina take the SR48 east following signs for the Passo Tre Croci for 8km to reach the top of the pass, and park on the right-hand side.

For a vehicle drop, take the SS51 north out of Cortina and follow this for 19km until the junction with the SP49. Turn right onto this, following signs for Misurina. After 1200 metres park the first vehicle on the right where the road crosses the Rio Val Fonda streambed. Continue in the second car along the SP49, passing through the village of Misurina to reach a T-junction. Turn right here and follow the road for a further 4km to reach the top of the Passo Tre Croci.

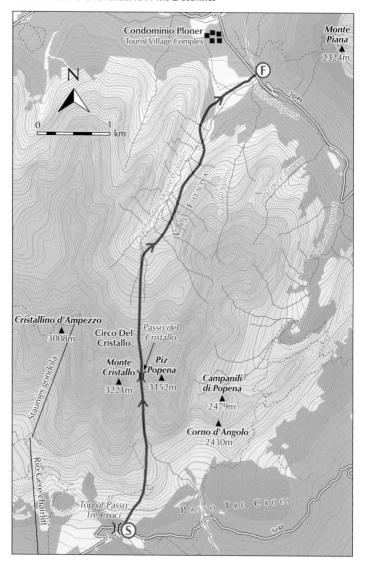

From the car park, cross the road to reach a signpost and information boards marking the top of the **Passo Tre Croci**. Don't follow the signposted paths and instead climb up the snow bank, ascending northeast and aiming for the gap between Monte Cristallo and Piz Popena, keeping to the less densely vegetated slope. Reach a vehicle track crossing horizontally over the path by a national park sign and turn right onto this, following it for 200 metres before ascending directly up a steep slope, making numerous kick turns. Reach and follow a blunt ridge, aiming for the obvious saddle of Passo del Cristallo between the peaks.

At the top of the ridge exit from the vegetation completely and enter into a bowl beneath the saddle. Traverse the bowl to the left, sticking above a band of small cliffs to enter into the main couloir. Follow this until a rocky outcrop splits the couloir; take the right-hand fork, aiming for a large boulder in the middle of the next couloir. The terrain now gets ever steeper and eventually requires removing skis and ascending the last 100 metres on foot, often using crampons, to reach **Passo del Cristallo**. Don't forget to turn around and admire the spectacular Sorapiss group before beginning the ascent.

From the saddle ski down the large open slopes of the **Circo del Cristallo**, often with great snow. Reach a change in gradient where the slope flattens above a series of rocky steps. Take the couloir just right of the valley floor which provides the only way down to the **Val Fonda**. Take care in bad visibility here if there are no tracks. Continue skiing carefully along several narrow passages.

This leads to a slope above a rocky ravine, where it is best to traverse up high on the left or right (right is the more popular option) to return to the valley floor at the end of the canyon. Cross Rio Val Fonda, then follow the stream right to return to the road and the car. In spring there is a good chance of getting your feet wet crossing the stream.

Other possibilities

If the conditions aren't suitable for ascending the south side or if you only have a single vehicle at your disposal, the itinerary can be done as an out-and-back up to **Passo del Cristallo**, staying on the north side for the entire route.

ROUTE 49
Giro delle Tre Cime

Start/Finish	Chalet Lago Antorno (1880m)
Distance	18km
Total ascent	900m
Total descent	900m
Grade	F 2.2
Time	6–7hrs
Aspect of ascent	S/N
Aspect of descent	N/S
Map	Tabacco No 03
Parking	Chalet Lago Antorno car park: 46.5942, 12.26412

This is a long and for the most part technically unchallenging snowshoe in the stunning setting of the infamous Tre Cime, the quintessential icon of the Dolomites. Overrun with visitors in the summer, the opposite is true in the winter and you will often have the route to yourself. It requires an absolutely safe snowpack for traversing the west side of the towers; if this is not the case then it's better to retrace your steps from the north faces.

APPROACH

From Cortina take the SR48 signposted to Passo Tre Croci and follow this for 14km up and over the pass to reach a T junction. Turn left here for Misurina and drive through the village, continuing for 50 metres past the end of the lake to a junction. Here turn right, following a sign to the Tre Cime, and continue past a campervan park and a campsite. Drive up the road until reaching Chalet Lago Antorno (opposite the lake by the same name) and park in the spaces alongside the road.

The initial ascent follows the summer toll road to the Tre Cime. This is usually pisted, making for an easy if rather long ascent to reach **Rifugio Auronzo** in around 1hr 30mins. This can be avoided in peak season by taking a snowmobile instead.

From the rifugio, follow path 101 east as it contours below the south faces of the Tre Cime, passing one short exposed section right by the rifugio which requires some caution. After half an hour, reach a small chapel dedicated to Maria Ausiliatrice, a name given to the Virgin Mary and continue to **Rifugio Lavaredo** shortly after. Pass this on the left then ascend the large open slope to reach **Forcella Lavaredo** and the first classic view of the Tre Cime north faces. From here the white and red colours of Rifugio Locatelli can be seen to the north, an optional extension for those keen to extend the day.

Drop down from the saddle into the valley below (a cornice sometimes forms here so take care) and head east, following the line of blunt ridges that run under the north faces. Keep some distance from the towers to avoid any ice falling off the faces, as well as to appreciate a better view.

Pass **Cima Ovest** (the right-hand tower) and aim for the ridge above **Col Forcellina Rifugio**. A final west facing slope poses some difficulties as this is both steep and prone to unstable snow. If the snow is safe it is possible to traverse directly to **Forcella col de Medo**; if not it is better to descend down to the right into the valley below before ascending back up to the saddle. In good weather a fence on the saddle makes for a good reference point.

Once at the saddle and with the difficulties now behind, traverse more easily to return to Rifugio Auronzo and reverse the route back down the toll road and **Chalet Lago Antorno**.

Other possibilities

As the complete route is a long day, spending a night in the winter room of Rifugio Auronzo can be a useful way of making the most of the daylight hours.

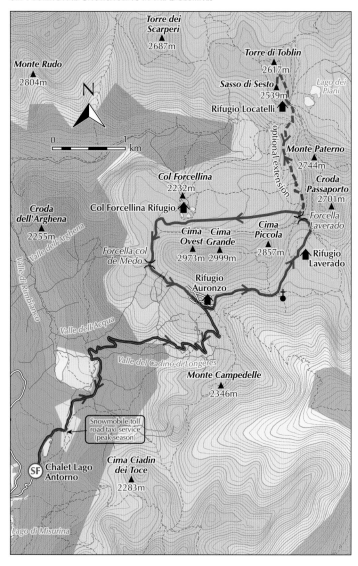

Below the iconic Tre Cime

The route can be extended by adding an out-and-back trip to **Rifugio Locatelli**, from where an easy ascent of the beautifully situated **Sasso di Sesto** (2539m) can be made (Route 50). This is a popular peak, which offers stunning views over to the north faces of the Tre Cime and a short but enjoyable descent.

For those wishing to avoid the slightly tedious initial part of the ascent to Rifugio Auronzo, there is a snowmobile taxi that runs during peak season from Lago Antorno (or occasionally from the first hairpin of the toll road).

ROUTE 50
Sasso di Sesto

Start/Finish	Hotel Dolomitenhof (1460m)
Distance	12km
Total ascent	950m
Total descent	950m
Grade	F 2.3
Time	4–5hrs
Aspect of ascent	E
Aspect of descent	E
Map	Tabacco No 010
Equipment	Ski crampons/crampons
Parking	Hotel Dolomitenhof car park: 46.66579, 12.35373

This popular ski tour ascends to the beautiful panoramic summit of Sasso di Sesto (2539m). The peak provides one of the best vantage points for viewing the iconic north faces of the Tre Cime and is best confronted in good weather to fully appreciate the stunning views the itinerary has to offer. The dramatic and easy to navigate Val Sassovecchio provides the meat of the route, often offering good powder snow.

APPROACH

From Cortina follow the SS51 to the north for 31km to reach the town of Dobbiaco in the Val Pusteria. Here turn right, following the SS49 for 4km before turning right again onto the SS52, now following signs Frocella del Tolp for Sesto (Sexten). Drive through Sesto to reach the town of Moos and turn right into the Val Fiscalina, signposted towards Bad Moos. Drive through Bad Moos to reach a parking area just short of Hotel Dolomitenhof at the end of the road.

From **Hotel Dolomitenhof** follow path 102 which heads south along tracks and various sections of cross country piste to reach **Rifugio Fondovalle** in 20mins.

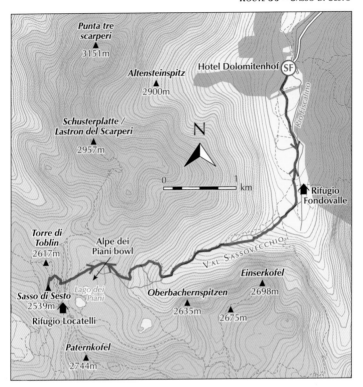

Continue following signposts for path 102 to bear southwest and head towards the easily identifiable Val Sassovecchio to the right. Enter the **Val Sassovecchio** and ascend the valley. It is more common to ascend the left side although either side is possible, so pick the easiest and safest way depending on the snow conditions; lookout for impressive icefalls too.

The valley is steep sided at first, necessitating a lot of traversing before the valley opens out and is barred by a set of rocky cliffs and often another impressive icefall. Avoid these by ascending the steeper slope to the right, choosing one of several possible shallow couloirs. Contour under the cliffs to the north, heading west and taking care to avoid several small ravines until reaching the large open plateau of the **Alpe dei Piani bowl** and the **Lago dei Piani lakes**, usually covered in snow during the winter months.

Stunning views from the summit of Sasso di Sesto

The pointy and distinctive tower of Torre di Toblin (2617m) is now clearly visible to the west. Aim just left of this, crossing the plain until Sasso di Sesto and the white and red building of Rifugio Locatelli come into view. Aim directly for the saddle between Sasso di Sesto and Torre di Toblin, accessed by a brief steeper section. Turn left and follow a wide ridge, usually on its left side, to reach the flat but beautifully situated summit of **Sasso di Sesto** with superb views in all directions.

To descend ski down your uphill tracks following the best snow.

Other possibilities
It is possible to link this route with the Giro delle Tre Cime (Route 49), although the logistics of the return will need to be considered.

APPENDIX A

Glossary of mountains, towns and passes

Below is a list of the more commonly used Italian and German names used throughout the Dolomites.

Mountains and groups

Italian	German
Alpe di Suisi	Seiser Alm
Catinaccio	Rosengarten
Cinque Dita	Fünffingerspitze
Marmolada	Marmolata
Odle	Geisler
Piz Boè	Boespitze
Punta Grohmann	Grohmannspitze
Sass de Putia	Peitlerkofel
Sassolungo	Langkofel
Sassopiatto	Plattkofel
Sass Rigais	Geislerspitzen
Tre Cime	Drei Zinnen

Towns and passes

Italian	German
Badia	Abtei
Bolzano	Bozen
Brunico	Bruneck
Campitello	Kampidel im Fasstal
Canazei	Kanetschei
Cortina d'Ampezzo	Hayden (obsolete)
Corvara in Badia	Kurfar/Corvara
Dobbiaco	Toblach
La Villa	Stern
Longiarù	Campill
Ortisei	St Ulrich
Passo Campolongo	Campolongopass
Passo Costalunga	Karerpass
Passo Falzarego	Falzaregopass
Passo Gardena	Grödnerjoch
Passo Giau	Giaupass
Passo Pordoi	Pordoijoch
Passo San Pellegrino	Sankt-Pelegrin-Pass
Passo Sella	Sellajoch
Passo Staulanza	Staulanzapass
Passo Valparola	Valparolapass
Pieve di Livinallongo	Buchenstein
Pozza di Fassa	Potzach im Fasstal
San Cassiano	Sankt Kassian
San Martino in Badia	Sankt Martin in Thurn
San Virgilio	St Vigil
Santa Cristina	St Christina in Gröden
Selva di Val Gardena	Wolkenstein in Gröden
Sesto	Sexten

APPENDIX B
Glossary of mountain terms

Italian	German	English
ago	Nadel	needle, pinnacle
alpe, malga	Alp	alp, upland meadow
alta via	hohenweg	high level path
alto	hoch	high
arva, pala e sonda	LVS-Gerät, Lawinenschaufel, Lawinensonde	transceiver, shovel and probe
attacchi	Bindungen	bindings
attrezzato	klettersteig	protected
baita	Berghütte	mountain hut
bastoncini	Stöcke	poles
bianco	weiss	white
biglietto	Fahrkarte	ticket
bivacco	Biwak	bivouac hut
bocca	Sattel	pass, saddle
bocchetta	kleine Scharte	small pass, gap
bosco	Wald	forest
cabinovia, telecabina	Gondelbahn	gondola lift
caduta di sassi	Steinschlag	rock-fall
camere libere	Zimmer frei	rooms to let
canale	Rinne	gully
canalone	Schlucht	gorge
carta	Karte	map
cengia	Band	ledge
chiuso	geschlossen	closed
ciaspe/ciaspole/ racchette da neve	Schneeschuhe	snowshoes
cima	Spitze	summit
col, colle	Hügel	hill
corda	Seil, Kabel	rope
cresta	Grat	ridge
croce	Kreuz	cross
croda	Felswand	wall, cliff
curve di livello	Hohenlinien	contour lines
destra	rechts	right

Italian	German	English
difficile	*schwierig*	difficult
diritto	*geradeaus*	straight ahead
discesa, giu	*absteig*	descent, down
dislivello	*Hohenunterschied*	altitude difference
esposto	*exponiert*	exposed
est	*osten*	east
estate	*Sommer*	summer
fiume	*Fluss, Strom*	river
forcella	*Scharte*	gap, small pass
frana	*Erdlawine*	landslide
funivia	*Seilbahn*	cablecar
fuori pista	*abseits der Piste*	off-piste
ghiaio	*Schutt, Geroll*	scree
ghiacciaio	*Gletscher*	glacier
ghiaccio	*Eis*	ice
gradini	*Klammern*	stemples, iron rungs
grande	*gross*	large
gruppo	*Gruppe*	massif, group
impianti	*Aufsteigsanlagen*	lift system
lago	*See*	lake
lavina/slavina	*Lawine*	snowslide
lontano	*weit*	far
marcia	*Tritt*	foot-hold
montagna	*Berg*	mountain
mugo	*Latschen*	small pine bushes
nebbia	*Nebel*	fog
neve polverosa/ neve fresca	*Puderschnee*	powder snow
nord	*norden*	north
noleggio	*verleihen*	to hire
occidentale	*westlich*	western
orientale	*östlich*	eastern
ovest	*westen*	west
parco naturale	*Naturpark*	natural park
parete	*Wand*	wall, cliff
parcheggio	*parkplatz*	parking
passo	*Joch*	pass
pelli di foca	*Skifelle*	skins
pensione	*Gasthof*	guest house

Italian	German	English
percorso	*Wanderweg*	path
pericolo	*Gefahr*	danger
pericoloso	*gefährlich*	dangerous
piano	*Ebene, Hochfläche*	level ground, plateau
piccolo	*klein*	small
pista	*Piste*	piste
piz, punta	*Gipfel, Spitze*	summit
ponte	*Brücke*	bridge
rallentare	*langsam*	slow down
rifugio	*Hütte*	mountain hut
rio	*Bach*	stream, brook
ripido	*steil*	steep
rosso	*rot*	red
salire	*aufsteigen*	ascend
sasso	*Fels, Stein*	stone
scala	*Leiter*	ladder
scendere	*absteigen*	descend
sci	*Ski*	ski
scialpinismo	*Skibergsteigen*	ski mountaineering
sci escursionismo	*Skitouren*	ski touring
sci nordico/sci di fondo	*Skilanglauf*	cross country skiing
segnalazione	*Bezeichnung*	way-mark
seggiovia	*Sessellift*	chairlift
sella	*Sattel*	saddle
sentiero	*Fussweg*	footpath
sinsistra	*links*	left
soccorso	*bergrettung*	rescue
strada	*Strasse*	road
sud	*suden, sud*	south
tempo	*Wetter, Zeit*	weather or time
torrente	*Sturzbach*	mountain stream
traversata	*Uberquerung*	traverse
ultima	*letzte*	last
valanga	*Lawine*	avalanche
val, valle	*Tal*	valley
vedretta	*Gletscher*	glacier
vento	*Wind*	wind
via	*Weg*	way, route
vietato	*verboten*	not permitted

APPENDIX C

Useful transport and tourist information contacts

General
www.visitdolomites.com
Overview site of the Dolomites covering history, culture, sports and accommodation.

www.dolomitisuperski.com/en
The primary resource for skiing, winter and lift pass information.

www.dolomites.org
Overview site with a focus on accommodation.

www.accommodation-dolomites.com
Accommodation search resource.

Tourist information
Val di Fassa
tel +39 0462 609500
www.fassa.com

Val Gardena
tel +39 0471 777900
www.valgardena.it

Alta Badia
tel +39 0471/836176
www.altabadia.org

San Martino and San Vigilio
tel +39 0474 501 037
www.kronplatz.com/en/san-vigilio

Val Fiorentina
tel +39 0437 720243
www.valfiorentina.it

Cortina and Misurina
tel +39 0436 866252
http://cortina.dolomiti.org

Taxi companies

Canazei and Arabba
Taxi Autosella
tel +39 0471 790033

Desilvestro Taxi e Viaggi
tel +39 335 760 5170

Taxi Arabba
tel +39 339 705 7095

Ortisei and Selva
Viaggi Gardena
tel +39 0471 795150

Taxi Val Gardena Taxileo
tel +39 335 841 0330

Corvara
Taxi Vico Alta Badia
tel +39 335 611 6528

Taxi Corvara
tel +39 339 881 7965

San Martino
Autoservizi Bruno Tavernaro
tel +39 0439 68227

San Cassiano
Taxi Renato
tel +39 345 639 3680

Selva di Cadore
Radio Taxi
tel +39 0436 860888

Taxi Roby
tel +39 328 712 8813

Pecol
Dolomiti Autonoleggio Taxi Alleghe
tel +39 340 679 6016

Cortina and Misurina
Taxi Cortina Sci
tel +39 338 488 9793

Taxi Cortina Autonoleggio con
Conducente
tel +39 335 637 1419

Bus companies
Cortina Express
tel +39 0436 867350
www.cortinaexpress.it
In addition to offering airport transfers,
it offers local services between Cortina
and the Alta Badia.

Dolomiti bus
tel +39 0437 217111
www.dolomitibus.it
Public service serving the Belluno and
Cadore regions.

Sad bus
tel +39 0471 450111
www.sad.it
Public service serving Bolzano,
Brunico, the Alta Badia, the Val
Gardena and Cortina.

Sudtirol Mobil
tel +39 0471 551 155
www.sii.bz.it/en
An online timetable resource for local
bus services within the Dolomites.

Trentino Trasporti Esercizio
+39 0461 821000
www.ttesercizio.it
Public bus service serving the Val di
Fassa, Val di Fiemme and Passo San
Pellegrino regions.

Airport transfer services
www.altoadigebus.com
Transfer service from Munich,
Innsbruck, Bergamo and Milan airports.

www.busgroup.eu
Transfer service from Milan, Bergamo
and Munich airports.

www.cortinaexpress.it
Transfer services from Treviso and
Venice airports.

APPENDIX D
Ski schools, mountain guide offices and sports shops

Ski schools

Canazei and Arabba
Scuola Italiana di Sci Canazei
Marmolada
tel +39 0462 601211
info@scuolascicanazei.com

Scuola Sci e Snowboard Arabba
tel +39 0436 79160
info@scuolasciarabba.com

Scuola Sci e Snowboard Dolomites
Rèba
tel +39 0436 781442
info@scuolascidolomitesreba.it

Ortisei and Selva
Ski and Snowboard School Ortisei
tel +39 0471 796153
info@scuola-sci.com

Corvara: South Badia
Ski and Snowboard School Dolomites
tel +39 0471 844018
lavilla@skidolomites.it

Cross Country School Alta Badia
tel +39 339 8068111
info@scuolafondo.it

Ski and Snowboard School La Villa
tel +39 0471 847258
info@scuolascilavilla.it

Ski and Snowboard School Badia
tel +39 0471 839648
info@scuolascibadia.it

Ski School Ladinia Corvara
tel +39 0471 836126
info@scuolascicorvara.it

Ski and Snowboard School Colfosco
tel +39 0471 836218
info@scuolascicolfosco.it

San Martino: North Badia and Fanis
Scuola Italiana Sci Sporting
tel +39 0474 501448
info@skisporting.com

San Cassiano
Ski and Snowboard School San
Cassiano
tel +39 0471 849491
info@scuoascisancassiano.it

Selva di Cadore and Pecol
Ski School Civetta Zoldo
tel +39 0437 788827
info@scuolascicivetta.it

Scuola Sci Val Fiorentina
tel +39 0437 720248
scuolasciselva@valfiorentina.it

Cortina and Misurina
Scuola Sci Cristallo Cortina
tel +39 0436 870073
info@scicristallocortina.com

Scuola Sci Cortina
tel +39 0436 2911
info@scuolascicortina.it

Mountain guide offices
Alta Badia Guides (Corvara)
www.altabadiaguides.com

Proguide (Corvara)
www.proguide.it

Guide Alpine Scuola di Alpinismo
(Cortina)
www.guidecortina.com

Association of Mountain Guides (Val
Gardena)
www.gardenaguides.it

Guide Alpine Dolomiti (Val di Fassa)
www.guidealpinedolomiti.net

Guide Alpine Val di Fassa (Val di Fassa)
www.guidealpinevaldifassa.com

Guide Tre Cime (Misurina)
www.guidetrecimedilavaredo.it

Cosley and Houston Alpine Guides
(International)
www.cosleyhouston.com

Sport shops

Canazei and Arabba
Amplatz SportAmplatz Sport
Via Dolomites, 109
38032 Canazei
tel +39 0462 601605

Sport Samont
Via Boè, 26
32020 Arabba
tel +39 0436 79142

Ortisei and Selva
Sport Gardena
Strada Rezia, 110
39046 Ortisei
tel +39 0471 796522

Sport Bruno Riffeser
Via Meisules, 131
Selva di Val Gardena
tel +39 0471 795141

Corvara: South Badia
Sport Kostner
Str Col Alt, 97
39033 Corvara in Badia
tel +39 0471 836933

Sport Tony
Strada Colz, 56
39030 La Villa
Badia
tel +39 0471847622

Cortina and Misurina
K2 Sport
Via Cesare Battisti, 32
32043 Cortina
tel +39 0436 863706

APPENDIX E
Further reading

Books

A Complete Guide to Ski Touring and Ski Mountaineering: Including useful information for off-piste skiers and snowboarders, Henry Branigan: AuthorHouse 2006

Avalanche Essentials: A Step by Step System for Safety and Survival, Bruce Tremper: Mountaineers Books 2013

Backcountry Avalanche Safety: Skiers, Climbers, Boarders, Snowshoers, Tony Daffern: Rocky Mountain Books 2009

Backcountry Skiing: Skills for Ski Touring and Ski Mountaineering (Mountaineers Outdoor Expert Series), Margaret Wheeler, Martin Volken, Scott Schell: The Mountaineers Books 2007

Ciaspolando in Alto Adige: Tappeiner 2011

Ciaspolando nelle Dolomiti: Tappeiner 2013

Freeride in Dolomiti, Francesco Tremolada: Versante Sud 2009

Scialpinismo a Cortina d'Ampezzo, Stefano Burra, Luca Galante: Idea Montagna 2014

Scialpinismo in Dolomiti, Enrico Baccanti, Francesco Tremolada: Versante Sud 2013

Scialpinismo in Val di Zoldo, Stefano Burra, Leonardo Pra Floriani: Idea Montagna 2014

Ski Touring: Essential knowledge for off-piste, backcountry, ski tourers and ski mountaineers, Bruce Goodlad: Pesda Press 2015

Staying Alive in Avalanche Terrain (2nd edition), Bruce Tremper: Mountaineers Books 2008

The White War: Life and Death on the Italian Front, Mark Thompson: Faber & Faber 2009

Websites and DVDs

First-Timer's Guide to Snowshoeing, www.snowshoemag.com/first-timers/
BMC Off Piste Essentials DVD: British Mountaineering Council, 2008

NOTES

IF YOU ENJOYED THIS GUIDEBOOK
YOU MIGHT ALSO BE INTERESTED IN...

Related titles

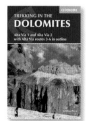
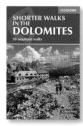
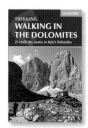

visit **www.cicerone.co.uk** for more detail
and our full range of guidebooks

LISTING OF CICERONE GUIDES

BRITISH ISLES CHALLENGES, COLLECTIONS AND ACTIVITIES

The Book of the Bivvy
The Book of the Bothy
The End to End Trail
The Mountains of England and Wales: Vol 1 Wales
The Mountains of England and Wales: Vol 2 England
The National Trails
The UK's County Tops
Three Peaks, Ten Tors

UK CYCLING

20 Classic Sportive Rides in South East England
20 Classic Sportive Rides in South West England
Cycling in the Cotswolds
Cycling in the Hebrides
Cycling in the Lake District
Cycling in the Yorkshire Dales
Cycling the Pennine Bridleway
Mountain Biking in Southern and Central Scotland
Mountain Biking in the Lake District
Mountain Biking in the Yorkshire Dales
Mountain Biking in West and North West Scotland
Mountain Biking on the North Downs
Mountain Biking on the South Downs
The C2C Cycle Route
The End to End Cycle Route
The Lancashire Cycleway

SCOTLAND

Backpacker's Britain: Northern Scotland
Ben Nevis and Glen Coe
Great Mountain Days in Scotland
Not the West Highland Way Scotland
Scotland's Best Small Mountains
Scotland's Far West
Scotland's Mountain Ridges
Scrambles in Lochaber
The Ayrshire and Arran Coastal Paths
The Border Country
The Cape Wrath Trail
The Great Glen Way
The Great Glen Way Map Booklet
The Hebrides
The Isle of Mull

The Isle of Skye
The Skye Trail
The Southern Upland Way
The Speyside Way
The Speyside Way Map Booklet
The West Highland Way
Walking Highland Perthshire
Walking in Scotland's Far North
Walking in the Angus Glens
Walking in the Cairngorms
Walking in the Ochils, Campsie Fells and Lomond Hills
Walking in the Pentland Hills
Walking in the Southern Uplands
Walking in Torridon
Walking Loch Lomond and the Trossachs
Walking on Arran
Walking on Harris and Lewis
Walking on Jura, Islay and Colonsay
Walking on Rum and the Small Isles
Walking on the Orkney and Shetland Isles
Walking on Uist and Barra
Walking the Corbetts Vol 1 South of the Great Glen
Walking the Corbetts Vol 2 North of the Great Glen
Walking the Galloway Hills
Walking the Munros Vol 1 – Southern, Central and Western Highlands
Walking the Munros Vol 2 – Northern Highlands and the Cairngorms
West Highland Way Map Booklet
Winter Climbs Ben Nevis and Glen Coe
Winter Climbs in the Cairngorms

NORTHERN ENGLAND TRAILS

A Northern Coast to Coast Walk
Hadrian's Wall Path
Hadrian's Wall Path Map Booklet
Pennine Way Map Booklet
The Coast to Coast Map Booklet
The Coast to Coast Walk
The Dales Way
The Pennine Way

NORTH EAST ENGLAND, YORKSHIRE DALES AND PENNINES

Great Mountain Days in the Pennines
Historic Walks in North Yorkshire
South Pennine Walks

St Oswald's Way and St Cuthbert's Way
The Cleveland Way and the Yorkshire Wolds Way
The Cleveland Way Map Booklet
The North York Moors
The Reivers Way
The Teesdale Way
The Yorkshire Dales: South and West
Walking in County Durham
Walking in Northumberland
Walking in the North Pennines
Walking in the Yorkshire Dales: North and East
Walking in the Yorkshire Dales: South and West
Walks in Dales Country
Walks in the Yorkshire Dales

NORTH WEST ENGLAND AND THE ISLE OF MAN

Historic Walks in Cheshire
Isle of Man Coastal Path
The Lune Valley and Howgills – A Walking Guide
The Ribble Way
Walking in Cumbria's Eden Valley
Walking in Lancashire
Walking in the Forest of Bowland and Pendle
Walking on the Isle of Man
Walking on the West Pennine Moors
Walks in Lancashire Witch Country
Walks in Ribble Country
Walks in Silverdale and Arnside
Walks in the Forest of Bowland

LAKE DISTRICT

Great Mountain Days in the Lake District
Helvellyn
Lake District Winter Climbs
Lake District: High Level and Fell Walks
Lake District: Low Level and Lake Walks
Lakeland Fellranger
The Central Fells
The Far Eastern Fells
The Mid-Western Fells
The Near Eastern Fells
The Northern Fells
The North-Western Fells
The Southern Fells
The Western Fells
Rocky Rambler's Wild Walks

Scrambles in the Lake District
– North
Scrambles in the Lake District
– South
Short Walks in Lakeland
Book 1: South Lakeland
Short Walks in Lakeland
Book 2: North Lakeland
Short Walks in Lakeland
Book 3: West Lakeland
The Cumbria Coastal Way
The Cumbria Way
Tour of the Lake District
Trail and Fell Running in the
Lake District

DERBYSHIRE, PEAK DISTRICT AND MIDLANDS
Dark Peak Walks
High Peak Walks
Scrambles in the Dark Peak
Walking in Derbyshire
White Peak Walks:
The Northern Dales
White Peak Walks:
The Southern Dales

SOUTHERN ENGLAND
South West Coast Path
Map Booklet –
Minehead to St Ives
South West Coast Path
Map Booklet –
Plymouth to Poole
South West Coast Path
Map Booklet –
St Ives to Plymouth
Suffolk Coast and Heath Walks
The Cotswold Way
The Cotswold Way Map Booklet
The Great Stones Way
The Kennet and Avon Canal
The Lea Valley Walk
The North Downs Way
The Peddars Way and Norfolk
Coast Path
The Pilgrims' Way
The Ridgeway Map Booklet
The Ridgeway National Trail
The South Downs Way
The South West Coast Path
The Thames Path
The Thames Path Map Booklet
The Two Moors Way
Walking in Cornwall
Walking in Essex
Walking in Kent
Walking in Norfolk
Walking in Sussex
Walking in the Chilterns
Walking in the Cotswolds

Walking in the Isles of Scilly
Walking in the New Forest
Walking in the North
Wessex Downs
Walking in the Thames Valley
Walking on Dartmoor
Walking on Guernsey
Walking on Jersey
Walking the Jurassic Coast
Walks in the South Downs
National Park

WALES AND WELSH BORDERS
Glyndwr's Way
Great Mountain Days
in Snowdonia
Hillwalking in Shropshire
Hillwalking in Wales – Vol 1
Hillwalking in Wales – Vol 2
Mountain Walking in Snowdonia
Offa's Dyke Path
Offa's Dyke Map Booklet
Pembrokeshire Coast Path
Map Booklet
Ridges of Snowdonia
Scrambles in Snowdonia
The Ascent of Snowdon
The Ceredigion and Snowdonia
Coast Paths
The Pembrokeshire Coast Path
The Severn Way
The Snowdonia Way
The Wales Coast Path
The Wye Valley Walk
Walking in Carmarthenshire
Walking in Pembrokeshire
Walking in the Forest of Dean
Walking in the South
Wales Valleys
Walking in the Wye Valley
Walking on the Brecon Beacons
Walking on the Gower
Welsh Winter Climbs

INTERNATIONAL CHALLENGES, COLLECTIONS AND ACTIVITIES
Canyoning in the Alps
The Via Francigena
Canterbury to Rome – Part 1
The Via Francigena
Canterbury to Rome – Part 2

EUROPEAN CYCLING
Cycle Touring in France
Cycle Touring in Spain
Cycle Touring in Switzerland
Cycling in the French Alps
Cycling the Canal du Midi
Cycling the River Loire
Mountain Biking in Slovenia
The Danube Cycleway Volume 1

The Danube Cycleway Volume 2
The Grand Traverse of the
Massif Central
The Loire Cycle Route
The Moselle Cycle Route
The Rhine Cycle Route
The River Rhone Cycle Route
The Way of St James
Cyclist Guide

ALPS – CROSS BORDER ROUTES
100 Hut Walks in the Alps
Across the Eastern Alps: E5
Alpine Ski Mountaineering
Vol 1 – Western Alps
Alpine Ski Mountaineering Vol 2
– Central and Eastern Alps
Chamonix to Zermatt
The Tour of the Bernina
Tour of Mont Blanc
Tour of Monte Rosa
Tour of the Matterhorn
Trail Running – Chamonix and
the Mont Blanc region
Trekking in the Alps
Trekking in the Silvretta and
Rätikon Alps
Trekking Munich to Venice
Walking in the Alps

PYRENEES AND FRANCE/SPAIN CROSS BORDER ROUTES
The GR10 Trail
The GR11 Trail – La Senda
The Mountains of Andorra
The Pyrenean Haute Route
The Pyrenees
The Way of St James – Spain
Walks and Climbs in the Pyrenees

AUSTRIA
The Adlerweg
Trekking in Austria's Hohe Tauern
Trekking in the Stubai Alps
Trekking in the Zillertal Alps
Walking in Austria

BELGIUM AND LUXEMBOURG
Walking in the Ardennes

EASTERN EUROPE
The High Tatras
The Mountains of Romania
Walking in Bulgaria's
National Parks
Walking in Hungary

FRANCE
Chamonix Mountain Adventures
Ecrins National Park
Mont Blanc Walks

For full information on all our
guides, books and eBooks,
visit our website:
www.cicerone.co.uk

Walking – Trekking – Mountaineering – Climbing – Cycling

Over 40 years, Cicerone have built up an outstanding collection of over 300 guides, inspiring all sorts of amazing adventures.

 Every guide comes from extensive exploration and research by our expert authors, all with a passion for their subjects. They are frequently praised, endorsed and used by clubs, instructors and outdoor organisations.

All our titles can now be bought as **e-books**, **ePubs** and **Kindle** files and we also have an online magazine – **Cicerone Extra** – with features to help cyclists, climbers, walkers and trekkers choose their next adventure, at home or abroad.

Our website shows any **new information** we've had in since a book was published. Please do let us know if you find anything has changed, so that we can publish the latest details. On our **website** you'll also find great ideas and lots of detailed information about what's inside every guide and you can buy **individual routes** from many of them online.

It's easy to keep in touch with what's going on at Cicerone by getting our monthly **free e-newsletter**, which is full of offers, competitions, up-to-date information and topical articles. You can subscribe on our home page and also follow us on **Facebook** and **Twitter** or dip into our **blog**.

Cicerone – the very best guides for exploring the world.

CICERONE

2 Police Square Milnthorpe Cumbria LA7 7PY
Tel: 015395 62069 info@cicerone.co.uk
www.cicerone.co.uk and **www.cicerone-extra.com**